The Ghosts of Saratoga

A novel about the
Turning Point of the
American Revolution

Dave Dampf

&

Dave Ossont

Milford House Press
Mechanicsburg, Pennsylvania

MILFORD HOUSE
an imprint of Sunbury Press, Inc.
Mechanicsburg, PA USA

NOTE: This is a work of fiction. Names, characters, places and incidents are the product of the author's imagination or are used fictitiously, and any resemblance to actual persons, living or dead, business establishments, events or locales is entirely coincidental.

Copyright © 2019 by Dave Dampf & Dave Ossont.
Cover Copyright © 2019 by Sunbury Press, Inc.

Sunbury Press supports copyright. Copyright fuels creativity, encourages diverse voices, promotes free speech, and creates a vibrant culture. Thank you for buying an authorized edition of this book and for complying with copyright laws. Except for the quotation of short passages for the purpose of criticism and review, no part of this publication may be reproduced, scanned, or distributed in any form without permission. You are supporting writers and allowing Sunbury Press to continue to publish books for every reader. For information contact Sunbury Press, Inc., Subsidiary Rights Dept., PO Box 548, Boiling Springs, PA 17007 USA or legal@sunburypress.com.

For information about special discounts for bulk purchases, please contact Sunbury Press Orders Dept. at (855) 338-8359 or orders@sunburypress.com.

To request one of our authors for speaking engagements or book signings, please contact Sunbury Press Publicity Dept. at publicity@sunburypress.com.

ISBN: 978-1-62006-308-8 (Trade paperback)

Library of Congress Control Number:

FIRST MILFORD HOUSE PRESS EDITION: July 2019

Product of the United States of America
0 1 1 2 3 5 8 13 21 34 55

Set in Bookman Old Style
Designed by Chris Fenwick
Cover by Lawrence Knorr
Edited by Chris Fenwick

Continue the Enlightenment!

This book is dedicated to the teachers of my life – those that taught me to be a loving son, a reader of books, a proud father, and a good man. I have learned more from you than you have from me.

– David Dampf

To Pam, Kyle and Hayley who are the point of it all, and to all the brave souls involved in the Battles of Saratoga.

– David Ossont

Table of Contents

Chapter 1   Crown Point

Chapter 2   Ticonderoga

Chapter 3   Hubbarton

Chapter 4   Fort Ann

Chapter 5   Fort Edward

Chapter 6   Stillwater

Chapter 7   Neilson's Farm

Chapter 8   Battle of Freeman's Farm Part I

Chapter 9   Battle of Freeman's Farm Part II

Chapter 10   Aftermath

Chapter 11   The Day After

Chapter 12   Entrenchment

Chapter 13   Bemis Heights

Chapter 14   Battle of Bemis Heights Part I

Chapter 15   Battle of Bemis Heights Part II

Chapter 16   Surrender

"These are the times that try men's souls: The summer soldier and the sunshine patriot will, in this crisis, shrink from the service of his country; but he that stands it NOW, deserves the love and thanks of man and woman. Tyranny, like hell, is not easily conquered..." - Thomas Paine

The Crisis, December 23, 1776

Map

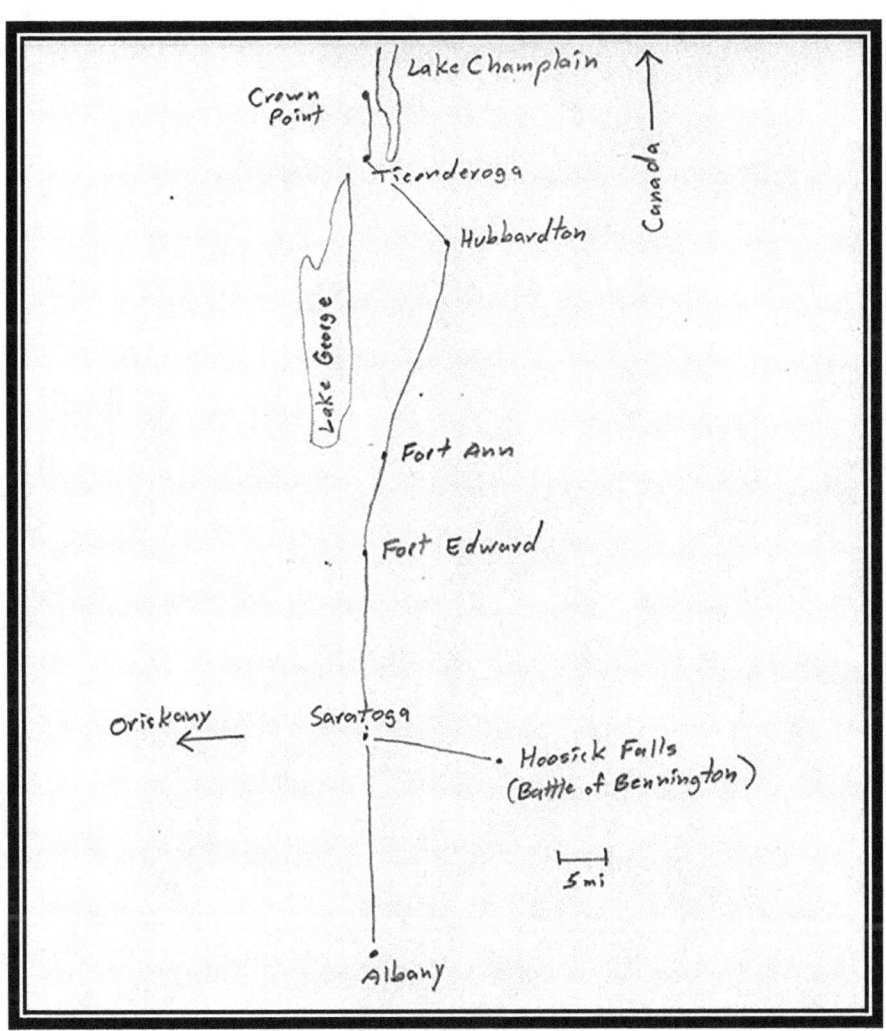

CHAPTER ONE – CROWN POINT

The mist hung heavy over Lake Champlain. From his watch post on the hill, Roland could not see the surface of the water, let alone the activity at His Majesty's fort at Crown Point. He could hear though. The British soldiers were up early, as they had been the last two mornings. That meant something was up and Roland figured it must have to do with General Burgoyne's army. General Schuyler, the head of the American Northern Department, was expecting a major invasion from Canada, no matter what anyone else thought. Some of the soldiers, mostly those from New England, didn't think much of him. Roland had great respect for General Philip Schuyler and so he too was a believer in an invasion.

Roland opened his haversack and rummaged for breakfast. A nice cup of tea with warm buttered biscuits would be lovely, he thought. However, that would require a fire and that would bring the Indian scouts down on him in seconds. The thought filled him with such dread he forgot all about a decent breakfast and settled for a bite of salt pork and a swig of water.

The late June sun was already heating the day and the mist was thinning. As the damp soil warmed, it gave off a thick smell of moss and decay. In this dense Adirondack forest, it seemed the leaves of a thousand autumns sat forever, never returning to the soil.

Overhead, some white-throated sparrows were flitting around the pine tree Roland leaned against. They called to each other, "*Sam. Pea-body*!" Roland closed his eyes and rested his head against the tree trunk. He had not slept well last night or any of the last three nights. Every time he nodded off; he woke to a dream of an Indian pouncing on him from the darkness. Often, he was roused, not by the dream, but by actual sounds of movement in the forest. The British and their Ottawa scouts were active in this area and more arrived every day.

A new rustling started as a breeze flickered the leaves of some nearby poplars. At the edge of his hearing another sound, something that didn't belong, joined in. At first, Roland couldn't place it. Straining to hear, he recognized the sound of paddles. It was the sound of hundreds of paddles dipping into the dark Adirondack waters. This was it!

He heard a snapping from behind, as of a twig being broken, followed by the soft rustle of brush being moved aside. Slowly and silently Roland moved his hand to his waist and pulled out his knife. Sounds continued from behind. He looked over to his rifle; too far away to reach in time. His pistol was near, but not loaded. Still, he might bluff the Ottawa with it long enough to get a running head start. Roland was fast; he might make it. In a single swift movement, he grabbed his pistol, leapt to his feet, and spun around, ensuring that he remained protected by the tree.

But it was no good, his arm now grabbed in a powerful grip and a hand clamped over his mouth.

"Not a word child, the danger's all around," whispered a deep voice.

The hands let him go. Before him stood a huge man, dressed in dark buckskin, rifle slung over his shoulder. His creased, weather-beaten face was unshaven, and he smelled of whiskey, but Roland's heart leaped to see him.

"Caleb! Thank God!" whispered Roland, trying not to shout with relief.

"Aye, Him too, I suppose."

"I think he's coming Caleb. Burgoyne. I can hear the paddles of bateaux, coming from the north. It sounds like it must be hundreds." Roland tried to keep the excitement out of his voice. He wanted to report like a seasoned scout, but his voice trembled as he waited for his grizzled sergeant to speak.

"I'll take you at your word, lad. Me old ears don't hear nothing. The Red men are about, we'd best be ready to move in a wink. Have you your spyglass to hand?"

"Yes, in my haversack." Roland made a move to get it.

"Not now, Rollie. The mist's rising, let's move on up to the top and see what we can see. Get your things and let's be gone." Even when he whispered, the Irish accent lilted over his words

Roland got his gear together. There wasn't that much, for a

scout traveled light. His cloth haversack held his food. His blanket, book, candles, and spyglass went into the knapsack which he strapped over his shoulders. Slinging his pouch containing the priming horn and bullets over his head, he tucked his pistol into the waist of his buckskin breeches. The threadbare cloth stockings were pulled up and the worn moccasins slipped over them. Whistling, he popped his three-cornered hat onto his head and cocked it to one side. He looked up and smiled at Caleb.

"You and your blasted hat." Them grenadiers'll use it as a target," growled the older man, but a smile played around his face and he slapped Roland on the shoulder as they moved up the hill.

The top of the hill was forested but Caleb and Roland had found a lookout two days ago when they first arrived at Crown Point. A tall pine tree, climbable by an agile young man made the perfect spot. Roland took his spyglass and worked his way up the tree. He was careful to keep plenty of the soft-needled boughs masking him from the fort, in case anyone glanced up.

The mist had risen from the lake and Roland had a good view. He could see down into the fort. The garrison gathered in formation on the parade ground. That meant something important. The fife and drum band were there too. The whole lot was prepared to march out of the fort. *For what?* he wondered. Then Roland lifted his spyglass to his eye and scanned northward up Lake Champlain. What he saw made him pull the spyglass away.

"Oh no, Caleb. Oh no."

"What is it, lad. What?"

They both were still whispering, and Roland's response was drowned out by the sound of the fife and drum band playing from the fort.

"Blast it boy, what the devil's going on?" His impatience was getting the better of his caution and Caleb's voice was loud enough to make Roland jump.

"It's as bad as it can be Caleb. It's unbelievable."

"Damn you, McCaffrey! Report! What do you see?"

This brought Roland back to the mission at hand. He calmed himself and spoke slowly.

"Sergeant O'Connor. It's the British flotilla... it looks like it's all of them. I can see bateaux, too many to count... a hundred or more I'd make it. Gunboats, a dozen, at least. Larger boats too, it must be frigates or something. Canoes and canoes of Indians and all the British soldiers in the world! Oh, Sergeant, it's bad as can be! It's..."

Roland stopped as the tree swayed. He grabbed at the nearest branch to keep from falling. He was astonished to see Caleb up in the tree with him. Upset about the British flotilla, Roland still couldn't help but wonder how Caleb had struggled his bulk up into the upper reaches of this tree. He could see the branch trembling under his sergeant's weight.

"Caleb?"

"You're right lad, it's not good." Caleb scowled out at the scene. Get your paper." Roland pulled out some crumpled sheets. He rummaged around in his pouch and found a piece of charcoal to write with.

"Write this down in columns... bateaux, gunboats, canoes, ships, cannon. See that tall tree on the opposite shore? The one with the dead mast? Each time a boat passes that spot, mark it in your columns. I'll try to see how many men are in each type of boat and maybe we can get some numbers for General Schuyler. Are you with me, boy?"

"I'm with you Caleb," replied Roland. Having a task had settled him down and put him back under control.

On the lake, a band had taken up a tune on one of the larger ships. They were playing "The British Grenadiers," a tune popular even with colonials. Caleb recognized the tune and exhaled.

"They'll not be playing that tune just for its beauty Roland. Take a gander."

Roland feared he would lose count, but, if Caleb was drawing his attention to it, he figured he'd better have a look. On the ship with the band were the biggest, tallest soldiers he'd ever seen. Each wore a tall, pointed bearskin hat. *Real Grenadiers*, thought Roland. *They're even more impressive than I'd imagined.*

"They don't look that tough. They've got silly hats," he said out loud, trying to bolster his courage.

Caleb chuckled. "Aye, that's true enough. And the next boat, do you see those men?" Roland put his glass on them. These men were in blue uniforms, with pointed helmets and most had huge mustaches. A short, fat officer paced on the top deck.

"Who's the fat man, Caleb?"

"That, my boy, can only be Baron von Riedesel, with his bloody Hessians. Burgoyne's brought his King's mercenaries to our fair land. This is serious business then, Hessians and Fraser's Grenadiers."

Hessians! Thought Roland, and a chill ran over his body. Hired by the British from German noblemen, the Hessians worked for blood money. What villainy they would do for the money had been proven at the Battle of Long Island. There they had bayoneted American troops trying to surrender. Their reputation as fierce and merciless fighters was known on both sides of the Atlantic.

"Keep counting, lad!"

Roland jumped and turned back to the flotilla to keep his tally. He thought of Caleb as the best man in America besides his father, but he wished he wouldn't always call him "lad" and "boy" and "child." Roland was already sensitive about his age, seventeen, and he didn't need to be reminded of it. The other scouts never let him forget anyway, with their constant jokes about him not shaving and how they could have him sneak into an enemy camp dressed as a woman. Still, Roland had heard Caleb address Major Whitcomb as "darlin'" from time to time. At least he hadn't used that on him yet. Even though a sergeant, it seemed like Caleb said whatever he wanted to whomever he wanted. Roland decided it would be hard to argue with anyone that massive, even if you were an officer.

Roland had been assigned to work with Caleb since the day he arrived at Fort Ticonderoga. Sergeant O'Connor was a burly, gruff Irishman. He liked to drink whiskey and, whether drinking or not, liked to curse about officers and Englishmen whenever the topic arose. He had served as a scout for the British during the war with the French and had spent time in the wilderness as an Indian fighter, against the Delaware. Great shocks of red hair poked out from under his coonskin hat and he seemed to have a permanent growth of whiskers on his face, even after shaving. His chest spanned like a beer barrel and his arms were as thick as Roland's legs. But the most prominent features were his hands. Callused and hairy, they were twice the size as a normal man's. He could pick up a cannonball with one, and Roland had the unsettling feeling that if he wanted, could crush it into dust.

The day passes unnoticed as Roland and Caleb counted the flotilla. It was an impressive show. By the day's end, Roland had tallied up over 200 bateaux, 400 canoes, 28 gunboats, and half a dozen larger ships. Caleb said there had to be over 5,000 men and 100 cannons. The high point came when the flagship passed, with General "Gentleman Johnny" Burgoyne on board. He stood out from the other officers, proud and handsome. It was easy to spot him, even without the spyglass, but Roland took a good peek through it anyway. *"If I were only on the shoreline, I could end this invasion right now, with one good shot,"* he thought, as the ship edged up to the fort. But even from the top of the hill, they could see the shoreline crawled with Indian and Tory scouts.

When darkness fell, they ate their pitiful supper. Caleb fortified himself against the night with two long swigs of whiskey. Before dawn, they planned to sneak down to the waterline and make off with one of the canoes. It was risky, but this news had to get to General St. Clair at Fort Ticonderoga as fast as possible. Without question, this was *the* British invasion and Fort Ti, mighty Fort Ti, barred their way. The British had no choice but to lay siege to it. Caleb reckoned this flotilla could move as early as morning, that meant time was all-important and travel by water was much faster than fighting your way through these forests and mountains.

Roland was having his fitful sleep when Caleb shook him awake.

"It's time, child. Remember, not a sound. They'll be everywhere. We must away and have a jump they can't make up, understand?"

Roland nodded. "I'm ready," he lied. Roland was a crack shot, considered one of the best in Fort Ticonderoga, if not in all New York, but he'd never shot at a man. If it came to that, he wasn't sure if he could do it. It seemed to Roland that you'd have to hate a man to kill him. While he hated "the British," or at least thought he did, "the British" were still an idea, not real people to him. No, he wasn't at all certain he could look a man in the eyes and shoot a lead ball through his body. But now...

Darkness was setting in as they moved down the slope towards the fort. Roland had spent many nights wandering the woods, it was his element. He had eyes like a cat, the darkness didn't slow him. He led the way, with Caleb following. Roland marveled at the swift and silent movement of the big man. He resembled a huge black bear moving along behind him but made less noise than the snowshoe hare that bounced across their path.

The fort itself rested on Crown Point, a peninsula that protruded into Lake Champlain. Roland and Caleb had been watching from a hill on the western side of the lake. They were separated from the fort by a small bay, one benefit of their site, since the water gave them distance from the fort but allowed them to see what was happening. However, it also meant that tonight they would have to travel around the bay to get to the channel leading to Fort Ticonderoga. Every extra minute they had to spend meant greater chances of encountering some of the Indian scouts who now, by Caleb's reckoning, numbered around 400. Still, this was the only way.

After creeping down a ravine behind the fort, they could see the water's edge. Now they had to find a two-man canoe. Moving so slow it hurt, they inched along until they came upon five canoes pulled up on the bank. Their owners were nowhere to be seen, but they couldn't be far off. Crawling on their bellies, Roland and Caleb moved up to the canoes. Caleb pointed to the one furthest downstream, Roland nodded and crawled toward it. He was almost there when he noticed that Caleb wasn't with him. To his surprise, he saw Caleb rise and deliver a savage kick to one of the other canoes. It made a terrible noise, emphasized by the silent night. *He'll raise the guard! What's he doing?* thought Roland. To his horror, Caleb ran to another canoe and again kicked it in. Now Roland could hear footfalls from the woods nearby. Still, Caleb did not come. Instead, he bent, picked up another canoe and, with a grunt, tossed it out into the water. Then he ran toward Roland.

Roland leaped into the canoe and moved it out into the water. Looking back, he could now see two Indians pursuing Caleb. Quick as the huge man moved, he would not beat them to the canoe. As the first Indian moved in, Roland shouted.

"Caleb! On your right!"

Caleb swung to his right, bringing up his rifle barrel as he did. The barrel deflected a ferocious blow from the Indian's tomahawk. Without a moment's hesitation, the big Irishman brought up the stock of his rifle. It hit the side of the Indian's head with a sickening crunch and the man flew off his feet. But now the second Indian moved on Caleb. As he finished his charge, Caleb flung his rifle. The Indian dodged, but it delayed his charge, and, by the time he recovered Caleb was crashing through the water to the canoe.

Roland was kicking up waves with the paddle by the time Caleb jumped into the canoe. He dared a look back at the landing. More than a dozen men were now along the shore, some Indians, some who appeared to be Tories- at least they weren't in British uniforms. A couple of men were swimming for the canoe Caleb had tossed into the lake. One of the other canoes wallowed in the water, the Indians not having noticed the damage from Caleb's kick. Men running along the wooded shoreline were shouting. Roland worried that they might get close enough to take a shot. Several men were now on the water in the undamaged canoe.

The canoe seemed to jump out of the water. Roland almost fell out and turned to see the piles of water being churned up by Caleb's paddle. In the front of the canoe, his massive shoulders were propelling them forward as though they were riding a wave. Roland fell to work again, and soon they were pulling away from the men running along the shoreline. The men in the other canoe, however, were also powerful paddlers and not easy to outdistance. In the canoe, a man raised a gun and the crackle of gunfire made Roland jump and paddle even harder.

"How close?" shouted Caleb over his shoulder.

"I don't know. I'm not hit at least," said Roland.

"No, I mean how close that canoe is?"

Roland twisted his head around. "200 yards I'd say. But we're holding them off."

"Shoot the man in front."

"What?" replied Roland in disbelief.

"I said shoot the man in front. I can't keep this pace up much longer. Don't worry, they've got muskets, they'll never hit you."

"How do you know?"

"I can tell by the sound. Now go on lad, I'll keep us straight while you shoot."

"Caleb..."

"Do it! Now!"

Roland laid down his paddle. He grabbed up his rifle and twisted around in the canoe. His heart was pounding, and he was still shaking from the effort of paddling and the excitement. He pulled the trigger without taking careful aim, shooting at the shapes of the men behind him. The shot ran wide. Roland saw the bullet splash into the water.

"I missed, Caleb." moaned Roland.

"Well damn it child, don't miss again. Me bloody arm's comin' off!"

Now it's a race against time Roland thought to himself. *Can I load and fire before they're on us?* He pulled his powder horn from his pouch and poured priming powder into the pan of his rifle. He could almost feel the enemy as he poured the measured powder down the rifle barrel. As he pulled the greased cloth patch from his rifle stock, he could hear another crack of musket fire and the plink of the musket ball hitting the water. *A bad shot* he thought.

Roland glanced back at the pursuing canoe. The man who had shot was kneeling in the middle of the boat reloading his musket. In seconds, he would be reloaded. Muskets were fast to reload. Roland had seen some men get off three shots in a minute. Reloading a rifle was a slow process. But once ready, the accuracy was excellent, in the right hands.

Roland placed the patch over the barrel of the rifle, positioned the lead on the patch and used his ramrod to ram them down the barrel. As he pulled out the rod the musketman got off another shot. Again, the musket ball hit only water. But the pursuing craft had gained on them. Roland could hear the ragged breathing of the men in the canoe behind him. He raised his rifle. That first shot had been a wild reflex, without thought or plan. This time he'd had some the opportunity to think about it. *Am I ready to kill?* he thought to himself.

The moment of truth came and went. Later Roland wasn't sure there had been any thought at all. The men in the canoe behind them were enemies. They would have killed both him and Caleb if they caught up. His friend and sergeant had almost been killed already. Roland took aim. His eyes met the eyes of the young Indian brave paddling in the front of the canoe. He appeared to be near Roland's age. He looked a little like some of Roland's Oneida friends back at the Fort. The brave never stopped paddling. His eyes widened right before Roland's rifle bullet struck him in the head and killed him.

The Indian slumped forward, still holding the paddle. It acted like a rudder and the canoe careened off course, almost circling back before another man had pushed the dead man overboard and started the pursuit again. This time the chase was halfhearted, perhaps the man now in front thinking there might be another rifle shot. After a few minutes, the canoe turned around and headed back toward Crown Point.

Roland didn't see the canoe head back. He didn't see his victim heartlessly pushed out of the boat. Once he had seen his bullet strike home, he turned and picked up his paddle once more. Neither he nor Caleb spoke another word until they came into sight of Fort Ticonderoga. He paddled, silent, alone with his thoughts.

Now I am a soldier. Now I am a killer. Thou shalt not kill?

CHAPTER TWO - TICONDEROGA

Roland lay sleepless on his cot. He had not slept more than two hours since he and Caleb had arrived at Fort Ticonderoga. The news they brought had whipped the garrison into an excited state of siege preparation. Both British and Americans believed a direct assault on Fort Ti was impossible. Its mighty stone walls would stand up to even heavy cannon fire. Cannon on the fort itself could destroy a naval attack. The design of the fort, in the "French" style, made an infantry attack an act of suicide. A star-shaped design allowed men to be positioned in each of its points. Any charge would be caught in a crossfire. No, the British strategy had to be a siege, day after day of cannon fire, waiting for the fort to run out of supplies before relief could arrive. So General St. Clair had set the garrison into action as soon as Caleb had reported to Major Whitcomb and he to St. Clair.

Boot heels clicked on the great stone parapet as artillerymen hurried to ready their cannon. From the docks came the sounds of men loading and unloading cargo. On the parade ground outside the barracks window, the fife and drum corps were drilling, and Roland could smell the hot metal being worked in the blacksmith's shop as they made repairs to equipment and ran new lead for bullets.

When the British flotilla arrived the whole garrison of the Fort had come out to watch. The British force seemed even more impressive now than when he had first seen it. At first, the men at Fort Ti had believed Roland and Caleb were exaggerating the size of the British invasion. As the boats came and came Roland had seen their eyes grow wide and their faces tight. It was easy to see that even if they were, for the moment, safe, in the "Gibraltar of the North," they were outnumbered and outgunned. The atmosphere in the Fort turned tense.

Last of all, Roland had been restless since their return. He couldn't get the image of the dead brave out of his head. When he slept, he still saw the death replayed over and over, but the Indian's face changed into Caleb's, or Roland's brother, Big John, or sometimes into Roland's own face. Sleep hadn't been welcome, even though he was tired from the scouting and the hard paddle home.

Far above Roland, on the open parapet on the top of the fort, stood General Arthur St. Clair. One arm lay crossed over his chest. The other arm's elbow rested on his right wrist. His left hand cupped his face. Though the General stood straight and still, Colonel Long recognized this posture as one of worry. Seeing this, he hesitated to approach St. Clair but thought perhaps he could help.

"It is an impressive force, isn't it sir?" he said.

St. Clair didn't move. "It is indeed Colonel," he replied.

"Still, they don't dare come closer. The guns can blast them out of the water if they do. And only a fool would try to charge us. We only have to wait for reinforcements from General Schuyler. We can hold them 'til then."

St. Clair dropped his arms and clasped his hands behind his back. "Do you think so, Colonel?" He glared at Long. "Take a look yonder." He pointed up to the small mountain they called Sugarloaf.

Long followed his gaze. On the side of the mountain, he could see the red coats of British soldiers, many British soldiers. *What the devil are they doing there?* he thought. Then he remembered that Polish engineer, Thaddeus something, telling General Gates on one of his rare visits, to consider fortifying that hill. Long also remembered Gates' reply. He didn't think it would be necessary.

"General...?"

"I'm not sure either, Colonel, but I have a bad feeling about it," said St. Clair, shaking his head. "Please send my compliments to Major Whitcomb and ask him if he would join us here, will you?"

A few minutes later Major Benjamin Whitcomb, Chief of Scouts at Ticonderoga, joined General St. Clair and Colonel Pierce Long as they looked out upon the British flotilla. The British force could no longer be called a flotilla, as many infantrymen now swarmed the shorelines on both sides of the lake, wisely out of cannon range. St. Clair had a spyglass trained on Sugarloaf.

"Thank you for joining us Major. I wonder if you would observe the action on Sugarloaf Mountain," said St. Clair.

"I have already done so, sir. Truth be told, I had been rather expecting you to be sending for me."

"You're a good scout, Major, always anticipating. Have you someone for the job? I'm afraid it may be most hazardous." St. Clair put down his spyglass and turned to Whitcomb, grave concern on his face.

Major Whitcomb threw back his shoulders. "Well, sir, I..."

St. Clair cut him off before he could continue. "No Major, I absolutely forbid it. I cannot afford to lose you, no matter how much I need to know what Burgoyne is up to."

Whitcomb seemed to sag. He kicked at the ground. "In that case sir, there are two men for the job."

St. Clair nodded. "I presume you mean those two who first brought us this wretched news. Are they rested enough for such a mission?"

"No sir, they are not. But is there any choice? I think we both have guessed what the British are doing and if we're right, you need to make some quick decisions before it's too late. O'Connor's the only one with a chance to make it there and back alive or uncaptured. And orders or no, young McCaffrey will go where O'Connor goes, even under threat of court-martial."

St. Clair looked up again at Sugarloaf, looked at the ground, then at Long and turned to Whitcomb.

"So be it Major." Whitcomb saluted and walked away.

Roland lay still staring at the ceiling. He was no longer sure he wanted to be a soldier. He wasn't sure if in the coming action he could point his rifle and kill another man again. And if he couldn't fight, he wasn't much use as a soldier. He needed advice; he needed to talk to someone. After all, he was seventeen, and just two months away from home. Why hadn't Caleb mentioned this? Now that he thought about it, he had not seen Caleb since they returned from Crown Point.

As this thought crossed his mind, Caleb walked through the door. Roland jumped to his feet.

"Sergeant!"

"Sit down lad, I'm come to talk. I can see you've not been yourself."

"Caleb, I've never killed a man before. That brave had his whole life ahead of him. Wife, children, grandchildren... all gone with a squeeze of my finger. I don't know if I can do it again, Sergeant. I don't know if I've got the belly to be a soldier."

"Ah! I should have known," rumbled Caleb, looking around the room,

"What else would it be?"

"Caleb, the British are here. There'll be real serious fighting soon. I don't know if I can do it. What good's a coward as a soldier? I'm useless." Roland tipped his head back and shouted at the ceiling. "What am I to do?"

He flopped down on his straw mattress. When he looked back, he saw Caleb sitting in a chair, sipping at his whiskey flask.

"Well, lad, you've said a mouthful there you have."

"How do you do it, Sergeant? How do you kill people without going crazy?"

Caleb chuckled and studied his flask. "Who says you don't go crazy?"

Roland looked at Caleb with eyes full of desperation. The big man leaned his head back 'til it rested on the wall. The coolness of the stone felt good on a hot afternoon in early July. He sighed and sat forward.

"Listen Rollie, I'm not much of a speechmaker. It's your Da should be tellin' you this, but he's not here. I know he's a good Irishman though, so maybe I won't be that far off the mark. Killin's a hard thing, a terrible thing. A man, a good man, has got to have good reason to do it. There's not that many things worth killin' for. Family...land...freedom." He laughed bitterly. "Good whiskey, though there's none about in this fair land."

"The British have long been our enemies, we Irish. I came to this wilderness to get away from them. But they brought their wars here, along with their laws. So, when it came down to them or the French, well, much as I hate to admit it, I fought for the bloody Brits. But I didn't fight to leave it to them to mess up. Men like General Washington and Mr. Franklin have made this a place worth something. A place where men can be free, where we can come and go and think as we please. I won't live in a land where the King tells me what to do, who to hate, who to kill and then taxes me for it."

Caleb leaned forward and took a long drink from his flask. Then he spoke again, this time almost in a raspy whisper.

"You came to be a soldier for your own reasons, Rollie. Only you know if those reasons still mean anything to you. If they do, you got to fight for them, for here we are, as you say, the British at our door. If those reasons were mere passin' fancy then you'd best away, and fast, for I've a bad feelin' in me bones concernin' this day." Caleb stood. "Major Whitcomb wants to see us. Clean up quick and report." He walked out of the room.

Roland pulled on his buckskin hunting shirt and tried to brush some of the grime off his breeches and stockings. *My reasons*, he thought, *my reasons*.

He remembered the argument when he told his parents he was off to join the army. It was his seventeenth birthday. Chores were done; supper finished, and his parents had presented him with a new tri-cornered hat.

"There's nothing for me here, Da. Big John's the farmer, you know that. I'm useless in the fields; crops die at my touch. My place is in the woods and the militia needs scouts. I can be somebody there!"

"You are somebody already! You're my son and if I say no, you won't go and that's that! shouted Evan McCaffrey at his middle son.

"You should be glad I want to fight the British. You've always said the only good Englishman is a dead one," pleaded Roland.

Evan looked at his wife, Molly. She gave him a stern scowl. "It's true, Molly, I have said that, and often. And well you know you feel the same way." He turned back to Roland. "Hate's a poor reason to offer up your life, boy," he said softly.

"But that's not the real reason, Da. *This* is the reason. "Roland held up a worn, dog-eared copy of the pamphlet by Thomas Paine, "The Crisis." He read out loud,

"'These are the times that try men's souls: The summer soldier and the sunshine patriot will, in this crisis, shrink from the service of his country; but he that stands it NOW, deserves the love and thanks of man and woman. Tyranny, like hell, is not easily conquered.' These are the reasons Da. I believe in these words Da. I feel them in here." He thumped on his chest.

The elder McCaffrey took the papers from Roland. He wiped his brow with the back of his hand. Evan looked at his wife and then back to Roland.

"Aye, it's true boy. They are good words, these. And fine men who wrote them. I believe in them myself. A man's got to fight for what he believes in this world, or else what's the point?"

The men turned to see Molly McCaffrey silently weeping into her apron. She raised her tear-streaked face to Roland and his heart broke.

Roland's memories were broken by a loud shout.
"McCaffrey!!!"
He grabbed his copy of "The Crisis" and raced off to Major Whitcomb's office.

Caleb was waiting outside the Major's door.
"Follow me in. Keep your trap shut. Don't offer to do anything, understand?"
Roland nodded.
Whitcomb looked up as they entered the room and made a sweeping gesture with his arm.
"O'Connor. McCaffrey. Please sit gentlemen."
"That's all right sir, we're well rested enough," said Caleb.
Whitcomb smiled. "I doubt that's true Sergeant, but as you wish. I'll get right to it; we've little time, I fear. The General and I believe the British may be moving guns to the top of Sugarloaf."
"But sir, no one could get cannons up them steep slopes, even

with a mule...aaah!" Roland was cut off by Caleb stomping on his foot.

"Hmm, that's what General Gates said as well."

Whitcomb stood and walked over to the window. His gaze drifted up to the side of Sugar Loaf. Even without his spyglass, he could see the red uniforms laboring up the slope. He turned again to the two scouts.

"However, there are some of us who feel it could be done. I don't need to tell you what the effect of a twelve-pounder on Sugarloaf would be."

"Why, they could fire right into the fort itself...ugghh..." Roland was again cut off, this time by an elbow in the ribs. Caleb glared at him. The Irishman spoke.

"We'll do it, sir. Me and the boy. We'll find out for sure."

"I hate to ask you Sergeant. You've just returned. But..."

"Begging your pardon sir, but you haven't asked. We've volunteered."

"Hmmn, yes. I see. Is that right, McCaffrey?"

Roland held up his papers. "It is for sure, Major. We ain't no sunshine patriots, me and Caleb... I mean, the Sergeant and I... I mean, yes sir."

Whitcomb smiled. "No, I'm sure you're not son. Nor summer soldiers, neither, I'd hazard. Good luck men. Be quick. Come direct to me on your return, no matter what time."

As soon as they were out of the major's office, Caleb smacked Roland on the head.

"I told you to keep quiet child."

"But he was asking questions," said Roland, rubbing his head.

"No, he wasn't. And besides, officers don't want to hear a soldier's opinions. They've always already made up their mind by the time they call you. Sunshine patriot, eh?"

"That's right, Caleb. I'd almost forgotten. These words, these words are my reason. They're why I'm here, and why I'll stay here, to fight."

"And kill?" asked Caleb.

"And kill." sighed Roland. He could feel his stomach tighten.

In the British camp, General John Burgoyne was getting anxious. This entire campaign had been his idea. British forces in North America had been altered to try his strategy to win the war. It was a simple idea and, in his opinion, beautiful. This was not too surprising, as Burgoyne thought everything, he did clever or brilliant. Having this opinion of himself, he also thought he deserved the best in life. He had brought along wagonloads of the best wine and champagne, the finest clothes and even his beautiful mistress. She was the wife of one of his men. If one led a war campaign it was still no reason to suffer.

Burgoyne's plan was three-pronged. It focused on Albany, New York, a major rebel stronghold. The Commander of the King's forces in North America, General Sir William Howe, already held New York City. He would move his forces north along the Hudson highlands. General Barry St. Leger would begin his eastward march in Oswego and travel through the Mohawk Valley, a hotbed of Loyalism. In Burgoyne's theory, once the British army came along, there would be thousands of Loyalists joining up as they moved toward Albany. Burgoyne himself led the north-south route from Quebec to Albany. When the three armies converged, they would take Albany without any problem. New England would be cut off from the middle and southern colonies. The rebels would be divided. "Divide and conquer" a tried and true military strategy, and it would work again, Burgoyne assured his superiors and King.

Now Burgoyne faced his first challenge, Fort Ticonderoga. It was a powerful and intimidating structure. Built with dirt and wood by the French and later reinforced with stone. In the Old French War, a garrison of 3,500 French troops had held off an attack by over 15,000 British and Americans. The next summer a British force under General Jeffrey Amherst had taken the fort in a vicious, bloody battle. It was then captured without a shot being fired when this rebellion had begun. It represented the first rebel victory. Benedict Arnold and some Vermont peasant named Ethan Allen had taken the entire British garrison by surprise in the middle of the night. Men at the fort had not yet heard about Lexington and Concord. The lone sentry had let the rebel army pass without question. The fort's commander surrendered in his nightshirt.

Both British and Americans believed that the fort could not be taken by a direct attack. Burgoyne himself had expected to lay siege to her for weeks. But once they had arrived and reconnoitered the area, General Phillips had come to him. Phillips trembled with excitement.

"General Burgoyne, the fools have left the door open!"

Burgoyne stared with impatience. Sure, that timing was everything in this campaign, he didn't want to wait here in this wilderness while they lay siege. "Come Phillips, you needn't be overly dramatic. Just tell me."

Phillips seemed hurt by the General's tone but continued. "Do you see the tallest mountain? That one there, which the locals call Sugarloaf."

"Yes, I see it," said Burgoyne.

"Well General, I have been there. The rebels have not fortified it. There's nothing there, not so much as a look-out!"

Burgoyne studied the mountain, now with greater interest. "Do you mean to say they have left the top of that hogback overlooking their fort unoccupied?"

"That is what I mean to say, sir." Phillips smiled with pride, now convinced that Burgoyne could see the brilliance of his idea.

"Phillips, can you...?"

"I can sir," Phillips interrupted. "Where a goat can go a man, can go. And where a man can go, he can drag a gun."

"What do you propose?" asked Burgoyne, becoming excited, despite himself.

"Two twelve-pounders, sir. With those, we can reach right into the fort. They'll have no defense. We'll shoot right over those mighty walls and cut them apart where they live."

"You may begin, General. You have my permission to take whomever and whatever you need."

"Thank you General, consider it done."

Burgoyne thought fast. If Phillips hauled cannon onto the top of that ridge he could fire right into the interior of the fort. General St. Clair would realize this too, thought Burgoyne. Perhaps he would surrender the fort and its garrison without a battle. That would add room to his timetable. Burgoyne could scent victory.

On July 5th, Burgoyne was waiting for word from Phillips. His latest report said the guns should be in place by sundown, perhaps sooner. One way or the other, the battle would soon commence.

Roland could not believe his eyes. Dozens of British soldiers were digging a road to the top of Sugarloaf. It was steep. In places, it looked like they were making stairs. But they were making good progress and behind the diggers were dozens more hauling two large cannon up the "road." The brawny Englishmen hauling the cannons were sweating and cursing in the summer heat

Roland dared to stand, trying to keep the thick hemlock tree between him and the work detail. Looking back, he could see right into the fort. He could see men out on the parade ground, and more at the docks, loading or unloading from several bateaux. He imagined he could even see General St. Clair standing out, pointing up at him.

Caleb touched his shoulder. Raising his arm at the elbow, he pointed, and Roland followed his finger. One, an Ottawa scout moving in their direction, acting suspiciously but not looking at them. Two, another Indian, coming behind them, checking near the bushes where Roland and Caleb passed. Three, a Tory scout with a rifle, watching the Indians and peering into the deep woods with his hand shielding his eyes from the sun. Four, a work detail with shovels headed toward these trees, maybe to get out of the hot sun for a while. Roland put his hand to his rifle, but Caleb leaned in close, his lips touching Roland's ear.

"No chance. Too many. Diversion and run." he whispered. Roland nodded.

Caleb reached back and pulled out his tomahawk. He studied the layout of men and forest for a moment. Then, catching Roland's eye, he tipped his head toward a thick tangle of brambles that had grown where some large pines had fallen down.

Roland nodded and crouched, ready for action. Caleb stretched back and heaved his tomahawk at a tree in the opposite direction of the brambles. It seemed to move in slow motion as it looped once, then a second time and then buried itself in the tree with a loud "thwunk."

As the British and Indians turned to react to the sound, Roland and Caleb ran into the brambles as fast as they could. His buckskin shirt protected him, but Roland could feel the sharp brambles ripping into his face and hands and tearing at his already holey stockings.

Surprise was on their side, also they were running downhill. A musket shot crackled out and then another and balls zipped through the woods. But they were firing blind and were not much of a threat. Roland worried more that some fleet-footed Indian might be on their tail. After a short burst of speed, he chanced looking over his shoulder, both to see if Caleb was there and if they were being pursued. To his surprise, Caleb was no longer running, but sauntering along as if out for a pleasant walk.

"Well, I guess that explains a lot right there," said Caleb, "they *want* us to report what we saw. Must be they figure it's to their advantage somehow. Come on, let's report."

Their report created a major stir at the Fort. St. Clair called all his officers in to discuss the situation. Caleb stood beside Major Whitcomb.

"Gentlemen," St. Clair shouted," let me put it this way and see if we can come to some kind of agreement. There's no question that Burgoyne has put two twelve-pounders on Sugarloaf. As we all are aware, if they are still operable after being hauled up that mountain, those guns will have a free shot right into our fort. They'll blast us with bombs, batter our walls down from the inside out, and then walk through the rubble to take us. The entire garrison will be killed or captured. Does anyone see it another way?"

No one spoke. St. Clair glanced around the room. All his officers sat or stood with their heads down, silent. He pursed his lips and blew out a puff of air. Then he spoke again, not so loud this time.

"Then I see no alternative. We must abandon the fort. As valuable as it is, the men are more important. If we can escape with a fair number of our guns and a decent amount of supplies, we can be around to fight another day, when the circumstances are more to our favor."

St. Clair shook his head and looked down at the table. He knew what the world would say about him for abandoning the fort without a fight. He would be branded a coward at best and a traitor at worst. But if he delayed there would be two problems. First, if those cannons were operable, the fort would be destroyed, and the garrison killed or captured. Second, if Burgoyne was as good a strategist as rumor had it, he would plan on their retreat and try to block off their escape route to the south. St. Clair could feel the blood pulsing in his temples as he made the terrible but only reasonable decision.

"I want to begin the evacuation immediately after dark. Pass the word little by little, and only to those who need to know until we're ready to go. The fewer men that know, the less the chance of the British finding out. Colonel Long, you will take Dr. Thatcher with our sick and injured, and the supplies and cannon and go down the lake to Skenesboro. From there, move to Fort Ann and then Fort Edward. It is important that the cannon make it, that is your priority. We have the chain across the lake to hold back the British boats. That should give you plenty of time before they can pursue."

"I will take the main garrison, head toward Hubbarton and then switch south to Fort Edward. Colonel Francis, Colonel Hale and Colonel Warner will act as rear guard to cover our escape. Major Whitcomb, assign your scouts as needed. Gentlemen, let us make haste before even escape becomes impossible."

After his men had left St. Clair walked outside to scowl up at Sugarloaf. He sighed and continued to stare, hoping to see the cannon falling out of control down the steep slope and crashing into Lake Champlain. But even as he watched, he saw a puff of smoke, followed by the roar of a cannon. A moment later a cannonball smashed into and through a bateaux sitting at the dock.

The broken pieces of the boat sank in the lake. St. Clair realized that he, like all the other men, stood standing dumbfounded with his mouth hanging open. He straightened himself, looked down at a group of men and snarled, "Get back to your duties!" then turned on his heel and stomped inside to pack.

The evacuation was a nightmare. Packing in the middle of the night, St. Clair had ordered lanterns and torches kept to a minimum to avoid alerting the British. Half the men had no idea what they were doing, or where they needed to go. The fort hummed with much noise and confusion. Roland figured the British would be lined up in battle formation outside the walls by the time they left. Men, supplies, and cannon all were carried ashore along a bridge made from bateaux tied together. Roland teetered out in the middle of the "bridge."

"Careful," he said, passing an armload of muskets to the man next to him, "they're coming untied."

"Truth to tell," said the man, "I ain't too worried about the muskets right now. Them British'll figger this out soon enough. I ain't of a mind to be caught out here bobbing around in the middle of the water when the shooting starts. No place to hide."

A loud splash brought shouting and cursing. A case of ammunition had been dropped, along with the soldier ferrying it across. The precious ammunition had sunk, and the man was thrashing around in the water.

"Can't swim!" he called. In the darkness, Roland could make out the shape of a man's head and arms flailing. As he was standing to dive in, he heard a familiar voice growl from further along the boat bridge.

"Stand up you bloody fool, you're in the shallows," growled Caleb.

It took hours to evacuate the fort. At last Roland stood panting on the main parade ground with the other scouts. He looked around. All the torches had been left burning to fool the British and he could see the outline of the walls and the silhouette of the sentries who would be the last to leave. *My home for these last months and now I may never see her again.*

Major Whitcomb called his scouts together. Next to him stood Caleb, holding a torch to light the scene. The flickering flame cast menacing shadows on their faces. Both were grimy with the smudge of torch fire and salty streaks of dried sweat. All the men were tired from the loading and the real work had only begun. Whitcomb spoke with a calmness, but his face was drawn and intense.

"All right men, this won't be easy. We know the routes, but this time it's night. We've got the regulars to handhold and maybe before long Gentleman Johnny on our tail. Keep ahead of the main troops, but don't lose them in the dark. They're not used to traveling at night. We don't want a lot of shouting for scouts to tip the British. We've fooled them so far, but their Indians will be on our track as soon as they see the Fort's abandoned. Groups one and two, I want you with the Hubbarton movement. Three and four, go with the boats to Skenesboro. From there you'll move to Fort Ann and then to Fort Edward. Any questions?"

The men looked around at each other.

"Seems plain enough to me," said Caleb.

Whitcomb nodded. Caleb tossed the torch away. As it flew, the light cast giant shadows of the scouts against the thick stone walls of Fort Ticonderoga.

Burgoyne was informed at first light he had taken Fort Ticonderoga, the "Gibraltar of America", without raising a musket. He allowed a broad smile to play over his face; things were going well, very well, but not perfect. He studied his map.

"General Fraser, I want you and Baron von Riedesel to pursue and take the force that is retreating by land. I suspect they are moving toward Fort Edward by way of Hubbarton. General Phillips, you need to get this army moving down the lake. I want to capture their cannon before they can drag them out at Skenesboro."

He looked at his officers, "Let's go, gentlemen, I want to move. We need only a skeleton force at the fort. Our goal lies to the south and we are on a timetable." He waved his hand to dismiss his officers to their tasks.

Burgoyne sat back, pleased. *Ahead of schedule,* he thought, *how nice, how very nice.*

CHAPTER THREE - HUBBARTON

Roland was dead tired. General St. Clair kept pushing the main part of the garrison through the night well past Hubbarton. Roland and Caleb had been sent back to inform the rear guard to proceed with all haste. The orders given to Colonels' Francis, Hale and Warner had been to come along as soon as the British pursuit stopped. But as they bushwhacked their way back, it became clear to Roland and Caleb that the Americans had encamped for the night. They were almost back to Hubbarton before they came upon the camp. Caleb put his hand on Roland's shoulder and stopped at the sight of the encampment.

"There's no sentries," he said. He sounded stunned by the fact.

Roland looked around. "Well, maybe they have them all posted to the north. That is the direction the pursuit would come from."

Caleb rubbed his unshaven, grizzled face. "Maybe, but that's not standard. There should be sentries all around. Saints preserve us, we can just walk in. We could be anybody, spies, assassins, Burgoyne himself."

It's true, thought Roland to himself as they walked unquestioned into the camp. *They can't see us well, it's still dark. But no one's even paying attention to two armed men coming into camp.*

Along the horizon, to the east, the sky was brightening. It was still night, not yet dawn. Though no sentries were posted, the men *were* all up and some almost ready to break camp. Roland and Caleb walked past Colonel Hale's men. They were putting together breakfast. Caleb stalked about looking for Colonel Francis. St. Clair had made it plain he was anxious for the rear guard to catch up. He was none too pleased with having to send scouts back to hurry them up. Caleb spied what must be

Francis' marquee, the command tent, among the tangle.

"I'll give the Colonel the General's message, boy. See if you can rustle up some coffee or tea or anything hot that might wake me up." said grumbled Caleb. He also seemed weary. He and Roland hadn't had much sleep in the last four days and the disorganized retreat had made him even crankier than usual.

Roland watched his bull of a sergeant stalk away, the unkempt red hair sticking out, as always, from under the hat. "Hat" was a generous description. It looked more like some unknown animal had crawled onto Caleb's head and died there.

Roland was tired too, and despite Caleb's instruction, he stood gazing around the encampment. It was still too dark to see well, but he could hear a lot of activity from both the soldiers and the pre-dawn insects in the woods. He closed his eyes and listened. Sleepy soldiers were putting together what breakfast they could muster from the hastily packed supplies. Roland could hear grumbled complaints about the food, the hard ground, and the officers demanding too fast a march pace. From across the encampment, someone whistled an Irish planxty. The scent of coffee and something burning came to his nostrils. Roland opened his eyes again, heard his name being called, and jumped, surprised.

"McCaffrey! Over here!"

Roland saw a group of men from the First New York Regiment, the fife and drum band. Calling to him was Keegan Peck, an old family friend who also was stationed at Fort Ticonderoga. He carried no fife around this time, though. Instead, a musket was leaning against the tree next to the fire. For now, at least, these musicians were a part of Colonel Turbott Francis' infantry unit. Roland walked over.

"You must be done in, Roland," said Peck, "How far ahead is St. Clair?"

Roland frowned; the question made him nervous. The rear guard hadn't progressed as far from the fort as they should have. If the British were moving south with any speed, they would be on them by morning.

"Couple hours, Keegan. Have you been here long?"

"Not long enough," replied Peck, "hardly asleep 'fore they

rousted us again. Still, it felt good to stop. Here," he held out a smoking, charred lump to Roland, "have some firecake while I get you a taste of this deadly coffee."

Roland took the firecake with some hesitation. It was only food in the most general sense of the word. Cooking in the field was never too good. When you were on the run it went to plain disgusting. Firecake sat at the bottom of the list. It was nothing more than a glob of flour, salt, and water smeared on a rock and placed into the fire. When the firecake was peeled off what you had was always raw dough on one side and burnt crisp on the other. Roland bit into it, trying hard to swallow instead of spitting it out.

"No sign of the British then?" he asked another of the soldiers.

"No, Colonel Warner told us they must have stopped at the Fort. Our scouts haven't seen nothing."

"Sentries?" asked Roland, spitting out an indigestible bite of firecake.

"Once it got dark, the Colonels called 'em all in. Said they needed a rest too."

"Mmmmm," nodded Roland as he accepted a cup of coffee from Peck. "Thanks, Keegan. Do you think I could have another for my sergeant?"

"Sure, do you want a cake for him too?" asked Peck.

"Yes," said Roland smiling, "that's good of you Keegan, I'm sure he'd love one. We've been on the move all..." Roland stopped and his face froze.

"Roland?"

"Keegan, get your musket, there's something wrong." Roland threw the firecake to the ground and grabbed his rifle.

Peck looked around. "What is it, Roland? What's wrong?"

"The crickets...".

"But I don't hear any..." whispered Peck.

"I know," said Roland as he ran full speed toward Colonel Francis' tent.

"Caleb! Caleb!"

Caleb burst out of the tent before Roland got there.

"Boy, we're in camp, you've GOT to call me Sergeant!" he

growled at Roland.

Roland ignored him. "Caleb, they're here. The British. Close. Colonel..."

Colonel Francis glowered at the young man standing shaking and breathless before him. At the same moment, he remembered pulling the sentries last night. He had never reassigned them. The Colonel turned to Caleb.

"Sergeant?" he asked, but Caleb was already priming his rifle.

"To arms men, to arms!" Francis shouted at the top of his lungs.

No sooner were his words out than there came a volley of crackling musket fire from the area of Hale's troops. Roland looked across and saw what seemed like half of Hale's command fall to the ground, shot down in the middle of their breakfast. Another volley rang out and the entire camp fell into chaos. Officers were running and shouting, and soldiers were scrambling for their muskets. Roland stood, looking, first one way then another, bewildered by the confusion. He felt almost yanked off his feet as Caleb pulled him close.

"Where be they, lad? The British, where?" he shouted.

Roland came to full alert at the sound of Caleb's voice. "There," he pointed to a hill beyond Hale's troops, "and there," he pointed to the woods between Francis' camp and Colonel Warner's camp.

Caleb turned to relay the information to Colonel Francis. Francis, a quick thinker, and an able officer had already sized up the scene. He was shouting orders, trying to organize his men into a repulse. He turned to Caleb.

"Tell Warner we'll regroup on that high ground." He waved his sword toward a small, wooded rise and ran off shouting orders without awaiting Caleb's reply.

Caleb again pulled Roland close. The sounds of the battle were making it difficult to hear.

"Work your way to that ridge child. I'll bring Warner", he shouted. Roland ran toward the high spot when he heard Caleb again.

"Rollie!" Roland turned. "Watch yourself, it's Fraser's Grenadiers!"

As he worked his way through the tangle of men Roland was almost trampled by a group running at full speed. Most of them were unarmed and they weren't running towards the battleground, but away from it. Roland realized it Hale's troops, fleeing in panic from the skirmish. He couldn't believe they were running away!

There was no time to think on that now. Francis' men were all around him and they were working their way to the high ground while firing some wild shots in the general direction of the British. Roland fired too, not even aiming, firing off into a general area like a musketman would. As he did, he glimpsed the tall bearskin hats of the grenadiers. It was true, they were engaged with the most fearsome fighters in the British army.

"Riflemen, riflemen! Gather here!" He could hear Colonel Francis' voice from the top of the rise. *Riflemen! That means me, he* thought and charged to the spot.

Colonel Francis remained calm and collected. The sharp edge of panic had left his voice and even as musket balls zoomed by, his instructions came out clear.

"You've got to slow their advance until we can organize our skirmish lines. Ignore everything else and concentrate on that first line coming from the gap between us and the Vermonters."

Roland looked at the spot. That was where the main British force advanced. *This is it,* he thought; *time to kill or die.* He rammed home the rifle ball. *I choose to live!*

Roland sighted his rifle down the slope. *How to choose?* Then a grenadier raised his musket. The motion attracted Roland's eye and he aimed and fired. The man crumpled and fell. His companions never even hesitated but kept coming. They moved forward in organized ranks, almost as one living thing made of little red parts. *It's spooky, like they don't know fear,* he thought. Roland took a deep breath and reloaded.

He could hear increased noise behind him as Colonel Seth Warner and his Vermont men arrived at the hilltop. Roland hoped that soon he'd hear Caleb's Irish cursing nearby. He aimed again, but a musket ball smashed into the dirt next to him and he flinched. Again, he aimed and fired, and again a man fell to the ground. As he reloaded, a rifle shot rang out above him and he flattened himself to the earth. Caleb kneeled beside him and reloaded his gun.

"Didn't mean to scare you, lad," said Caleb, but from his stifled chuckle that wasn't true. Roland smiled and shook his head.

On the battleground, Colonel Francis' strategy was proving effective. The British front line was being mown down at an effective rate. The riflemen's deadly accuracy had almost stalled their progress. Colonel Hill, the British officer in charge of the attack, slowed his advance, thinking he had underestimated the rebel numbers. He now guessed there must be double the number his scouts had reported. He would have to reorganize the attack until Generals Fraser and von Reidesel caught up.

The hesitation was what Francis counted on. He and Colonel Warner formed their men into skirmish lines, one behind the other. Their men were well disciplined, and the countercharge assembled without delay. The riflemen fell back as the infantry took position. Their line of fire now blocked, Roland and Caleb could only wait as Francis prepared his men for the classic battle strategy.

At the officers' command, the first line of soldiers fired their muskets. Not bothering to aim at a specific target. A musket wasn't like a rifle. At a range of 100 yards, its accuracy could be off by 10 feet. With tactic, the idea was to fire as many musket balls into the enemy's ranks as fast as possible. The more lead flying around, the greater the chance it would hit somebody. Since the same strategy was used by both sides, battles waged separated by only 100 yards or less. Men would march shoulder to shoulder, advancing toward their enemy. At a certain point, one army would feel they had the advantage and would fix bayonets and charge. This fearsome hand to hand fighting was the way most battles ended, with one army routing the other from the battlefield.

From his position on the hill, Roland watched the American troops make their counterattack. As soon as the first line fired, they dropped to their knees and reloaded. The second line stepped up, fired and did the same. Then the next line, and by then, the first line had reloaded, and they stepped again to the fore. It was incredible to watch. The lines reloaded their muskets with great efficiency, firing three times a minute.

When this part of the battle began, there wasn't much for a rifleman to do but watch. It took at least three to five times as long to load a rifle and there wasn't any way to affix a bayonet. It would still be possible for a rifleman to pick off individual targets, but the muskets filled the air with thick smoke and Roland waited, afraid he'd hit one of his own men. Caleb, however, continued to fire.

"Caleb, how can you see anything?" asked Roland.

"The red sash on the officers," he replied, "aim for that."

Roland peered through the smoke. Sure enough, he could see the British lines well enough to see the crimson sashes the officers wore across their waists. The idea was they would help the men recognize their own officers in the smoke and confusion of battle. But it could work for the other side too, if the enemy had good snipers. Roland aimed and fired, but he couldn't tell if he hit his target.

"How can you tell if you hit anything?" he asked Caleb.

Caleb smiled, "You just got's to trust in God and the Continental Congress boy."

Down the hill, a shout went up as the American forces made a bayonet charge and drove the British into the woods. The charge stalled, however, and there followed increased musket firing from the British positions.

"Reinforcements," muttered Caleb.

Minutes later, the patriot infantry poured back up the hill. They were all sweating and breathing hard. It seemed to Roland that most of them had holes shot in their clothes, and half of them were bleeding from one or more wounds. A surgeon was running from man to man treating the most serious of injuries. The men were still reloading, but most of them were now sitting on the ground, tired. Their faces were caked with sweat and soot. Keegan Peck plopped to the ground next to Roland. His bayonet was fixed on the barrel and Roland could see the blade was coated with a sticky, shiny substance. *The blood of an Englishman.* thought Roland. Keegan lay back on the hillside and smiled over at Roland.

"Them Grenadiers be tough men Rollie. And I'm feared there be more coming,

I could swear I heard their band." He chuckled. "Sounded good, too. Fine pipers, the British."

"Are you hurt, Keegan?" asked Roland.

Keegan grunted and sat up. He started reloading his musket and turned to smile at Roland. His face was covered with soot from the musket. His eyes had been watering from the smoke and there were two streaks where his tears had made clean spots.

"Thank ye for asking Rollie, but no, I'm all right. Just tired."

They could hear Colonel Warner's voice booming. "Get ready boys, here they come!"

The British had their band playing a stirring march as they advanced out of the woods and formed into ranks. Not far from Roland, a nervous young soldier fired his musket, but the enemy was too far away, and the young man got a swift kick in the pants from his sergeant for his twitchiness. As he waited for them to get in range, Roland had to admire the British soldiers' discipline. They formed their ranks with precise, quick movements as they came into the open. Their advance stayed smooth and tight. It seemed there were twice as many redcoats as the last charge. There were too many ranks of Continentals in front of Roland for him to see what was going on, but he could hear the steady beat of the British drummers and hear the American officers calmly talking to their men.

"Steady boys, not yet. Let them get close, not yet."

A hand tapped Roland's shoulder. Beside him stood Corporal Steen, Colonel Francis' adjutant.

"Are you McCaffrey?" he asked.

"Aye," said Roland, puzzled.

"The Colonel wonders if you could shoot that artilleryman setting up the field piece at the edge of the woods."

Roland, still confused, replied, "I'm not sure I follow you, sir."

The corporal was becoming impatient. "You *are* McCaffrey?" he said again, this time louder.

Roland nodded his head to add to the truth of it. "Yes, but I don't understand why Colonel Francis wants me..."

By this time Caleb had come over to listen. He interrupted Roland and spoke to the corporal.

"By God, yes, he's McCaffrey and your Colonel's heard right, there's not a better shot north of Virginia. But how do you expect him to see, let alone shoot past all these men?"

Corporal Steen seemed shaken by the sudden appearance of the hulking sergeant. He stammered a little in his response.

"Oh, um, well you see, uh...Sergeant, I was going to suggest that he use that tree yonder." Steen pointed to a thick maple that rose above the back side of the hill. "I believe two strong men could boost him up and then hand up his weapon."

Caleb nodded and rubbed his cheek. "That's not a bad idea Corporal, not bad at all." He turned to Roland. "What do you think child? Can you do it?"

"Actually, Sergeant," said the Corporal," I believe Colonel Francis meant it more in the way of an order than a request."

Caleb patted the man's shoulder with his massive hand. "I'll keep that in mind, son. Never you worry." He glanced back to Roland. "Well, Rollie?"

"It's a long shot, Caleb, I mean Sergeant. Might take me a couple of tries."

"Well boy, if'n they get that piece goin' there'll grape shot cutting us all to pieces. Come on," Caleb said to the corporal, "let's get him up that tree."

Roland climbed to the top. The battle was heating up. He saw the British charge up the hill. The firing was constant; men were falling every second on both sides. For a moment it appeared the charge would work, but Colonel Warner's men put on a flanking movement and shattered the British line once again. They retreated, the veteran British soldiers appearing somewhat stunned at the ferocity of these ragged farmers. Francis reorganized his ranks as if he might charge the famous grenadiers.

As the battlefield cleared once more, Roland searched for the artillery piece. It was still hard, even from the tree, to get a good view. There were smoke and men and trees - in the way. At last, he saw a small cannon, a field piece, with several men preparing it for action. Two more guns were being hauled up and lots of blue uniforms were moving in the woods.

"Caleb, Sergeant, there's three pieces being set. And the Germans are here!"

"Germans?" called out Corporal Steen, "Are you sure?"

"Easy enough to recognize, sir, in those pointy hats. It's them," replied Roland." What do you want me to do Corporal? Corporal?" Roland looked down.

"He's gone, boy. Off to tell the Colonels the bad news, I guess."

"What should I do Caleb?" asked Roland.

"Get those artillerymen, lad. If they get those pieces goin' we're in trouble no matter what."

Roland squinted back at the British line. No question about it, the Germans were here, he could hear their band. They were playing a tune that made it sound like they were out for a Saturday night dance, not a war. And not only playing, but they were also singing! Roland felt his hair rise. He remembered the field piece. The artillery officer was ready now, giving the orders to fire. Roland aimed his rifle and whispered, Sorry."

The shot caught the officer right in mid-order. He fell against the barrel of the cannon, clutching his shoulder. His men hurried to help him, casting fearful glances up the hill. Even though he hadn't killed the man, Roland could see he'd disrupted the gun's team. They'd need a few minutes to recover. As he reloaded, he focused his attention on the next gun crew. The officer squatted down to sight in the gun. Roland knew he'd be a sitting duck for a few seconds. He aimed and fired. The shot hit the man in the face, tearing away one of his cheeks. He fell to the ground and Roland lowered his rifle and looked down. He took several deep breaths and reloaded. By the time he was finished, he could see the British advancing again, this time supported by German lines. Among the regulars, Roland spotted the fat German he had seen on the flotilla, Baron von Riedesel. Beside him was a British officer. Roland figured it had to be General Simon Fraser.

"They're coming, Caleb! All of 'em!" he shouted.

"Then get down here boy, we'll never stand another charge. Get ready to move fast."

Caleb was right. This time there were too many of them. The musket volleys took down dozens of Continentals. The British ranks stepped forward with practiced smoothness each round. Soon they would be close enough for a bayonet charge.

Warner's men were under attack by the German riflemen, the "jaegers." These troops were named after their weapon, the German jaeger. It was a gun similar to an American rifle but shorter and heavier. Every bit as accurate as a Pennsylvania long rifle but with a shorter range. The Hessian sharpshooters were skilled riflemen. At this distance, they were picking off the Vermont militiamen with ease. It was becoming suicidal to stay. Francis realized the danger.

"Retreat! Down to the bottom of the hill! "he shouted.

Men poured off the high ground, leaving behind the precious supplies and cannon. There was a fenced field at the bottom of the hill, and here the men slowed and took cover. Francis knew how important those supplies could be. The men were at the edge of panic. If he couldn't rally his troops all would be lost. He leaped to the fence.

"All right, boys. We've lost the high ground, but they're not ready for a charge. They think we've run to Albany. Form ranks and we'll push them back off that hill. We drove these bloody redcoats into the woods once. We'll do it again!"

The frightened men seemed to take courage from Francis. Even as they looked at each other uncertainly, they were clustering around him. Roland heard several bayonets being fixed into position. Francis continued pulling his men together.

"It'll be a while before those slow-footed dragoons can get to the top. It's just the British there now. Go in low and they'll shoot over us."

The Colonel's plan seemed sensible. Roland knew from experience how difficult it was to aim at a moving target above or below you. And the American infantry had moved the enemy off the field once already today. He stepped up to take a position in the charge. A large hand reached for him from behind and dragged him out of the ranks.

"Caleb! What are you doing? We're about to charge!"

Caleb didn't answer, but a stubby finger pointed out from the giant hand to the hill above. Coming over the top were ranks of British soldiers, bayonets fixed. They were moving fast, with

The Ghosts of Saratoga· 37

confidence, and it was plain they meant business.

"You see that, child?" said Caleb, "That's the best fighting unit in North America. They be comin' downhill, with bayonets fixed, in tight ranks. These here men won't be breakin' that charge, not this day."

Roland's eyes grew wide. Caleb was right. This advance intended to finish the Americans, down to the last man. If they charged uphill at them, they'd all be butchered. But Francis' courage had spread. The men rallied into position. Ranks were formed and officers had their men ready. Francis waved his sword to signal the charge. A rifle ball struck him in the chest, and he fell to the ground, dead on the spot.

This proved too much for his men to bear. At the sight of their fallen Colonel, they scattered into the woods in total disorganization. Caleb and Roland stood watching, unsure of what to do. Colonel Warner's voice again boomed above the din.

"Scatter and meet me in Manchester!" he shouted.

Caleb grabbed Roland by both shoulders and spun him around.

"Listen, boy, we've got to split up. I've got to get to the General, let him know how close the pursuit is. You're to head to Fort Ann, report to Colonel Long. Do you understand?" Caleb looked with fire into Roland's eyes. He'd never seen the big Irishman so intense. It gave him a scare and he could only nod.

"Then away, boy, fly!" he bellowed.

Roland turned and raced into the woods. Before the revolution, his family had farmed in this area for a while. He knew every trail, every stream, every road. There was no way the British army could ever catch him, he knew. *But how many of their Indian scouts are about?* he wondered. He considered a twisting, winding path to throw off any pursuit, but decided time was more important. His feet pounding, he set off on the most direct route to Fort Ann.

Two days, two battles, two defeats, he thought as he ran through the forest. *Is this the beginning of the end in our fight for freedom?*

CHAPTER FOUR - FORT ANN

On July 8, 1777, Roland came in sight of Fort Ann. Roland's spirits sank even lower when he saw this "fort." For starters, it was small. Even the insignificant force gathered there now had spilled out into the clearing around the decaying log structure. There were many more men in tents than the fort itself could ever hold. He could see no real stand could be made here, not against the powerful force Burgoyne commanded.

Roland trudged up to the tents surrounding the fort. The exertions of the past few days had caught up with him. Even though spurred by fear of pursuing Indians he had walked the last few miles. It was no longer possible for him to run. He figured he should report to command inside the fort. He shuffled that way when he heard his name called.

"Roland! Roland McCaffrey!"

Roland turned toward the voice. To his delight, he saw the familiar faces of the New York Militia under Colonel van Rensselaer. In this 400 strong group of men, he saw many old friends. It was one of them, his old friend and neighbor, Captain Peter vanBrocklin who called out to him. Roland smiled with relief but straightened himself, walked up to the Captain and saluted smartly.

"Captain van Brocklin, I have come from Hubbarton. Our forces under Colonels Francis, Warner and Hale were defeated by a force of British and Germans under General Fraser, part of General Burgoyne's invasion force. I am sorry to report that Colonel Francis is dead."

The smile vanished from the Captain's face.

"Francis dead? Are you sure Roland?" he asked.

"I'm afraid so Captain. I was standing nearby. We were routed and our forces scattered throughout the woods. Colonel Warner's men are to meet him in Manchester, but I don't know the

The Ghosts of Saratoga· 39

whereabouts of Colonel Francis' men or Colonel Hale's."

"And the main garrison from Fort Ti?" said van Brocklin.

"With General St. Clair. Sergeant O'Connor set off to warn them of the hot pursuit."

"I see. Well done, McCaffrey." said the Captain. Then, leaning close so no one else could hear, "I'm glad you are well, Rollie. When I learned you were at Fort Ti, I hoped to see you, though you look like the devil himself. I'll report your news to the Colonel. Go over and get some food and drink. We'll talk after I report. I see you still have the rifle."

The Captain slapped Roland on the shoulder and walked away.

"Begging your pardon, Captain..." Roland called after him.

vanBrocklin stopped and turned, tipped his head toward Roland.

"Captain," said Roland, "Nicholas... I mean... is he here, sir?"

The smile came again to the Captain's face. He turned back to his troops and shouted.

"Nicky!"

A young man came running from out of the group. He was dressed in the working clothes of a farmer. Roland's age, and a tall, burly boy. Yet he had the smiling, open face of someone who had never uttered an unkind word.

"Father? I mean Captain?"

The Captain nodded in Roland's direction and the younger man's eyes followed. He broke out into a great, broad grin and ran toward Roland. The Captain again strode away.

"Rollie," said Nicholas van Brocklin as he embraced his childhood friend, "I feared for your life when I heard of the invasion, fears well-founded from the look of you. Come, rest and eat." He put his arm around Roland and led him to the militia's cooking area.

"I'm well enough Nick. Unhurt, but tired and tired of death."

"I know what you mean. It's not as glorious as it seemed when we were children is it?" said Nicholas, shaking his head. The two sat down and Roland shrugged off his packs and accepted some tea, biscuits and even some venison. Several other friends of Roland's came over to hear about the evacuation of Fort Ti and the battle at Hubbarton.

The vanBrocklins were more than family friends. Roland was still a youngster when it became obvious to everyone that he had no interest or skill in farming. It wasn't that he didn't try but crops just died under his hand. His brother, Big John, needed only to toss seed on the ground to make it grow and flourish. Roland was more at home in the woods. His gift was for hunting, fishing, and woodcraft.

One day his father had asked him to walk with him to the next farm, the vanBrocklins'. Young Nicholas was one of Roland's best friends. His father, Peter, was already a respected officer of the local militia. He was also the area's best hunter, trapper, and fisherman. It was said of Peter vanBrocklin that he could find his way home blindfolded from Philadelphia.

"Rollie," said Evan McCaffrey when they had arrived, "I have made arrangements with Mr. vanBrocklin to take you on as apprentice."

"What?" said Roland in disbelief, "I thought that meant tradesmen?"

vanBrocklin laughed.

"So, master McCaffrey. You don't think what I do is a skilled trade, eh?"

"Well...I... it's just," stammered the youngster. "It's just that I think of it as fun. I could spend all day every day, in the woods and mountains. It's where I feel at home."

"It's where you *will* spend every day from now on, son," said Evan.

For the next three years, Roland had traveled with the elder vanBrocklin. From him, he learned to shoot, to trap, to throw the tomahawk. He learned how to track both man and beast and how to navigate by the stars or sun. He learned how to sooth the weather, how to read the land, and how to move silently in the woods. vanBrocklin became like another father to him. Not a replacement, for Roland still loved and admired his own father. Peter made an additional figure to look up to. The apprenticeship ended when vanBrocklin went off to serve as an officer in the Continental regulars.

Nicholas was like Big John, a born farmer. Though he would sometimes come along on the trap lines, Nicky couldn't keep up the pace set by his father in the woods. He was an easy-going, happy fellow with never a bad word for anyone. Many a time he had helped Roland to his feet and dusted him off after his Irish temper had led to a fight with a bigger boy. Now here stood Nicky, in the middle of this war, as out of place as Roland had been behind a plow. Still, it was good to see him again.

"I'm afraid I've got more bad news, Rollie," said Nick, after Roland had told his tale of defeat. "Colonel Long arrived here not long ago with the rest of your people from Fort Ti. The British caught up with them at Skenesboro. Many men captured and supplies lost. There's a British force under General Phillips on their way here even as we speak. Father and the Colonel have been trying to decide if we have enough men to go out against them."

Roland's shoulders drooped under the news. *More death,* he thought, *is this how my life is to be forever?*

Nick looked into his friend's eyes. "You're tired, Rollie. Why don't you lie down in my tent for a while? We'll wake you if anything happens."

Roland nodded, "I could use some sleep." He smiled. "It's good to see you, Nicky. Even under these conditions."

Nick laughed. "I'll even see if I can find you some stockings that aren't torn to shreds. You're still tough as they come, Rollie. At least I get to march on a road or a trail."

Roland laid back in the tent and in no time fell asleep. Perhaps because of seeing Nicky and the Captain, he dreamt of home.

There was his father, strong and hard-working, raising up a family in an unknown land. There stooped Big John, giving his gift of life to the crops, talking to the young shoots as they broke through the soil. There was his mother, always calm, soothing the tempers of her family. She was walking towards him now, something in her hands.

"What have you got, Mother?" he asked.

"Your gift," she said, holding out her hands.

"Gift? Why, it's not my birthday?"

"Not that kind of gift, Rollie. A gift like your brother's."

"His gift of life?" asked Roland, excited now.

His mother extended her hands and Roland pulled them open. He recoiled in horror. In his mother's hands rested a human skull.

"No, Rollie," she said with a smile, "the gift of death."

Roland bolted awake, his heart pounding. The sounds of the camp in action were everywhere. Nick came to wake him, complete with a new pair of stockings.

"This is it, Rollie. We're marching out to meet the British. Our scouts have found a ravine right along the route the redcoats travel. It's the perfect place for an ambush. Father wonders whether you'd like to join up with us, or work with your people from Fort Ti."

Roland paused to think. It would be some comfort to fight alongside his childhood friends. But then an image came to his mind of some of them lying dead at his side.

"I guess I'd better report to Colonel Long, Nick. Do you know where he's at?"

"I told Father you'd feel that way. Long's at the front, he's getting ready to disperse his troops now. You'd better hurry."

Roland pulled on his moccasins over his new stockings and put on his buckskin shirt, pack and battered hat. He took a deep breath and picked up his rifle and was ready to go. He paused for a moment.

"Nicky?" he said.

Nick paused from his own packing. "What is it, Rollie?"

"Just be... I just don't want to...take care, Nick." Roland said and ran off.

Nick watched Roland running toward the front of the camp. "You too, Rollie, you too," he said to Roland's vanishing form.

The ambush was not to be. The British had learned of the plan. When they came to the ravine, the enemy was already in battle formation. Still, the stage had been set and Colonel Long was anxious to make up for his losses at Skenesboro. He ordered the advance and his men moved forward.

Roland had been sent ahead with another scout to find a way to flank the enemy. From a small rise, he peered down the ravine. Drums beat out the advance on both sides. Waving above the New York militia's ranks was a flag Roland had never seen before. He pointed it out to the other scout, Owens.

"Is that their militia's flag?" he asked.

"Oh, no," said Owens, "that's the new flag of our country. The 'Stars and Stripes' I've heard they call it."

Roland looked again at the flag. He couldn't see it well through the woods, but sure enough, it had a series of stripes on it and in the upper corner some stars. *A new flag for a new country*, he thought.

No sooner had that thought crossed his mind than the battle commenced. At once Roland could tell that this British force was not cut from the same cloth as the men, he'd battled at Hubbarton. They weren't as well organized, didn't redress their ranks with the same skill and didn't seem to get off as many volleys as Fraser's company. Still, Roland feared for his friends as he and Owens maneuvered around the ravine trying for a flanking path.

They followed a small stream and found what they were looking for. This could be even better than flanking the enemy ranks. If vanRenssalaer's men could move fast and without making a racket, they could assault the rear of the British position. Roland and Owens raced back to inform Colonel Long.

Long couldn't pull the whole militia for the main battle. But here lay the opportunity he was hoping for and he had devised a plan.

"Captain vanBrocklin, move your men up the ravine to this flanking position. When you hear our attack, begin yours."

Roland led the militia. They were all men used to traveling through the woods with speed and silence. They moved along the streambed and into position. From their vantage point, they could see Long's troops, the British position, and the battle line.

vanBrocklin sent his men out into a long fishhook-shaped maneuver flanking and circling behind the British position. Roland took his place among them. A messenger was sent to Colonel Long, and in a few minutes, Roland could see the main American force advance.

It was a classic musket charge. One line after another fired, loaded and advanced. As they advanced, the shorter range brought them under heavy fire from the British and they wavered for a moment. Roland and the men around him were anxious to act. They could see their comrades decimated in the ravine. But Captain vanBrocklin was waiting. He'd noticed the British making a maneuver, one that would bring their entire left wing into the militia's killing zone if he could be patient.

vanBrocklin stood churning with impatience. Long's men were losing their discipline, faltering. But if he could hold on for a few minutes longer, it could turn the whole tide of the battle. He rose from his position to get a better look at the British. As he did, a group of crows in the trees above him flew from their branches, cawing. The sound of the birds caught a British scout's attention. He turned, saw vanBrocklin and shouted, "Flank! Flank!" vanBrocklin fired, and his entire company emptied their muskets as one.

The attack from their flank and rear caught the British off guard. A mass volley from the militia brought down most of the left wing. What remained of the British force reacted with a hasty retreat. They were fighting in unfamiliar territory with thicker woods than they were used to. The militiamen were taking full advantage of the trees as cover. As they continued to pour volleys into the British flank, the main American line advanced.

It was too much for the British. They were taking heavy losses and the Colonel commanding the force could see that the rebels would soon be in a position for a bayonet charge. He ordered a general retreat to a small hill behind their position, away from the murderous fire of the militiamen.

Although these infantrymen were not as tough as the grenadiers, Roland had to admire their battle savvy. The retreat was organized. A rearguard kept up resistance while the main force made its move. It remained smooth and without a touch of panic. He thought of the disorganized mess the Americans were in after Colonel Francis was shot at Hubbarton.

Before they could be broken, the British were once again in battle position, this time with the advantage of higher ground. For two hours the skirmish waged on. There was no way for the British force to escape, yet the Americans were unable to take the hill. Colonel Long was reluctant to risk everything on all-out charge; British reinforcements could turn up at any moment and flank him.

Losses were heavy on both sides. At last, the firing seemed to slow down and then stopped. Roland wasn't sure why but got his answer when he went to reload. He was out of bullets, and it was a good guess that everyone else was too. Orders came down the line for the militia to join the main group.

Colonel Long was furious. With ammunition running low, the loss of supplies at Skenesboro now loomed as a major disaster. By their lack of response, he reckoned the British were low too. If he still had that ammunition... It would be possible to make a bayonet charge, but much of his force was militia and they weren't skilled at hand-to-hand combat. Few militiamen even had bayonets.

The issue was decided when he heard war whoops coming from the road to Skenesboro. It had to be British reinforcements. The war cries would be from their Indian scouts. Long wasted no time. He wasn't about to lose his entire force to gain a brief victory. He ordered a retreat to Fort Ann.

Fort Ann turned out to be only their temporary destination. Convinced that a large British force, perhaps Burgoyne's main force, was on their tail, Long ordered a retreat all the way back to Fort Edward. The men gathered all the useful supplies they could from Fort Ann. As they left, the Americans set the fort on fire to prevent the British from using it.

Roland was more discouraged than ever. Despite a valiant effort, they had been unable to defeat the British- even when it seemed certain that victory was theirs. Instead, here he was, retreating again. He hoped General St. Clair waited at Fort Edward with the main garrison.

A weary Roland walked beside the creaky wagon that carried the wounded. Inside lay the bloodied, but still living body of his friend Nicholas. Roland had carried him from the battlefield himself. Dr. Thatcher was changing one of his bandages.

"Is he going to live?" asked Roland.

"Well, he's got numerous wounds," replied Thatcher," but he's not bleeding too much. Nothing time won't heal Roland, but he needs rest. You'd best be getting back to your unit."

"How long before he'll be able to talk?" asked Roland. He was reluctant to leave his friend.

"Come back in the morning, after he's eaten," said Thatcher.

Breakfast thought Roland, *that gives me the night to figure out how to tell him his father's been killed.*

CHAPTER FIVE - FORT EDWARD

General Burgoyne shook his head in disgust. In the days since his early and easy victories at Fort Ticonderoga, Skenesboro, Hubbarton, and Fort Ann, the campaign had soured. It had taken his force 21 days to cover the 23 miles from Ticonderoga to Fort Edward. It was unbelievable. And now, to see that the "fort" offered little more than a pile of rubble, was very discouraging.

Things had started unraveling when Burgoyne decided to take the land route southward. The way down Lake George would have perhaps been easier, and the roads were better. However, that route also had drawbacks. It would have been impossible to move the larger boats over to Lake George. The smaller bateaux could have made the trip, but they couldn't carry the larger cannon.

Of equal importance to the boat problem, he reflected, the Lake George route would have meant going back up to Ticonderoga, which would have looked like a retreat. After the surprise of the strong resistance the rebels had put up at Hubbarton and Fort Ann, he couldn't afford to give them any sign of weakness or indecision.

Without a doubt, his forces at Fort Ann would have been captured by the rebels had not that resourceful soldier scared them off with his ridiculous war cries. To think one man imitating an Indian battle cry could drive off the entire rebel force! It boggled the mind. He called to his aide.

"Send a bottle of wine to Baron vonRiedesel with my compliments. Bring me champagne and something to eat in my tent."

The aide ran off and Burgoyne walked to his tent and sat at his writing table. His head was throbbing, both from the aggravation of the day and from too much champagne the night before. Still, it was important that he get a letter off to General

Howe in New York to let him know the situation. He wrote:

Greetings my dearest General and esteemed friend,

I have, at long last, arrived this day of 28 July at Fort Edward. It is a fort in name only, as I would consider it useless as a place of defense. Since we last communicated, I have encountered numerous troubles.

Although it was St. Clair I routed from Ticonderoga, my true foe here has been General Schuyler, who, it turns out, is a clever fellow indeed. Once he heard of our success, he sent his spies and axmen into the woods in great number to bedevil me. I cannot number the trees they have felled in my path, but it seems half the forest blocked my progress daily. When we tried to avoid these barriers by following streams, we discovered that the rebels had rolled large boulders by the ton into every stream bed, making them impassable as well. My men have chopped enough wood to fuel all of London for a century.

When we were able to get through the woods and into some open areas, we found that Schuyler had diverted streams, his men were digging new watercourses and every open area and road was turned into a muddy quagmire. Men and wagons mired in the muck and caused further delay.

With all the delay, I had need of many times the food I had originally figured on. Thus, I was forced to send to Canada for more and had to again wait for its arrival. When I sent foragers into the area, they found that the inhabitants had driven off their animals, hidden all foodstuffs and even burned their crops, all to vex us. It is my understanding that Schuyler's wife herself set the torch to some of the fields. It has become quite plain to me that our Loyalist friends were overly optimistic about the support we would find among the people hereabouts.

This situation has not been helped by an extremely unfortunate incident which happened yesterday. A young woman from the area, a Jane McCrea, who was engaged to marry one of my Loyalist officers, was accidentally killed by one of our Indian guides. I, of course, was outraged and was going to have the savage executed. My hand was stayed when their leader told me that if I were to kill the man, all the others would immediately desert. Although the crime is repugnant, I have great need of the scouts and was left no choice. However, there is already a great hue and cry about the land, and I fear the Ottawas may run home despite my clemency.

I am wondering if you have heard of General St. Leger's progress through the Mohawk Valley. I hope he has been able to find more Loyalist support than I. By my estimate he should soon arrive at Fort Stanwix. As I have stated before, the timing is critical, and he must join his force with mine before we reach Albany.

I know you have your problems keeping track of that old fox, Washington, but again I implore you to send as many men northward as you can spare. Despite my recent problems, I am still on schedule and I have learned that Schuyler has fallen back all the way to Stillwater. I am optimistic that we can have this rebellion taken into hand by Christmas.

My best regards,

J. Burgoyne

Burgoyne folded the letter and sealed it with a few drops of wax. When his food arrived, he sent the letter off. The pounding in his head continued. The next few weeks would be crucial. With every day he moved south, it became harder and harder to keep the supply line flowing from Canada. His scouts had brought information saying large numbers of rebel militia were building up in Vermont and New Hampshire. The Tory support had never shown up in the number expected and if St. Leger didn't make it through the valley, Burgoyne could find himself deep in enemy territory on his own.

Still, every engagement had been a victory. And despite the slow journey to Fort Edward, there remained still plenty of time. The men were in good spirits, the wine holding out, and there was good company. He was confident his soldiers could defeat twice their number of these motley, ill-dressed, poorly-equipped farmers. He took a long drink from the glass and his headache faded.

CHAPTER SIX - STILLWATER, 1ST WEEK OF SEPT.

Caleb and the rest of Roland's messmates were working on the evening meal. Roland could smell it as he approached their fire area. Here at the Stillwater camp, the food was decent. There had been corned beef, rice, onions for stew, turnips, potatoes, and peas. Even better they had fresh bread every night and warm biscuits and coffee every morning. Twice there had even been tea, a rare treat in the colonies since the Boston Tea Party. Caleb surprised Roland by proving to be an able cook. The young rifleman reckoned by the smell he'd be eating mutton tonight.

It had been discovered that Roland had little talent in the area of cooking. To him fell the jobs of gathering firewood and finding news of the war. The latter job also fell to him as the only one of the six who could read. Roland didn't mind. Looking for firewood gave him some time alone. Ever since the death of Peter vanBrocklin he had felt like keeping to himself anyway. Gathering the war news helped him keep a positive outlook. It was encouraging to hear that other patriot forces were faring better than his group.

"Good news, boys," Roland said as he walked up to their mess area, "and lots of it!"

"Well don't tell us now," growled old Ben Hudson, "wait till we're relaxin' at our supper and can 'preciate it."

Roland smiled and shook the papers in his hand at Ben. "I swear Ben if you get any uglier or meaner, we won't be able to tell you from an old black bear sow."

"Why you little..." Ben jumped up and tried to cuff Roland with his open fist but Roland was too quick, and all the other men laughed, enjoying the show.

"All right!" boomed Caleb, "quit foolin' around you two. Slop's on."

After everyone filled their stomachs a little, Roland pulled out the two handbills he had traded from Corporal Harris in exchange for a cartridge box he had traded Sergeant Jones an antler-handled knife for. Nobody in the camp had any money. Trading was how all business happened. One of the regular jokes of the Continental army was getting paid. Congress claimed to be sending them all regular wages, but they never came.

"There's two here, one about Bennington and one for Oriskany. How do you want 'em?" asked Roland.

"Do like usual Rollie," said Johnny Cooper, another scout. "You pick out the important stuff and tell us in your own words. I can't ever understand what these educated men are trying to tell me."

Roland nodded and studied the papers while he gobbled a nice chunk of bread with some cheese and washed it down with some buttermilk, a real treat even here. He set down the cup and studied the report. The brittle paper crackled in his hand. It seemed all the paper had turned poorer quality these days. In the distance, Roland could hear a fiddler warming up. There was always music around the campfires.

"The first one's about Oriskany. I expect you all have heard the stories by now, but this here's the official story. On August 3, General Barry St. Leger, with a large force of Tories and Indians arrived at Fort Stanwix and demanded surrender. Our Colonel Gansevoort laughed in their face. The British laid siege to the fort, figuring to starve them out. But a messenger got through to General Nicholas Herkimer who raised up the Tryon County Militia to lift the siege.

At a place called Oriskany, the militia was ambushed by the Indians and Tories. The Indians were Mohawks under Chief Joseph Brant, so you know they were bad."

At this, the other men mumbled in agreement. The Mohawks were the largest tribe of the Iroquois nation. Joseph Brant was the Iroquois' greatest chief, tough, smart and merciless. His warriors would fight to the end, hand to hand if need be.

"The ambush caught the militia by surprise and General

The Ghosts of Saratoga· 53

Herkimer was wounded. But he had his men set his saddle up on a hill and he directed the battle from there, while he smoked his pipe.

The militia was able to regroup and put up a terrific fight. The fighting was close, much of it was hand to hand. Tomahawks, knives, bayonets, and muskets used as clubs. It's being called the bloodiest battle of the war. It says here that men were even killing each other with their bare hands. The only time the fighting let up was during a bad rainstorm.

Our boys put up more of a fight than the Indians were ready for. After the rain, they pulled out. Without their red friends, the Tories had no belly for fighting and they retreated too. But the militia had lost too many men to help at Stanwix, and they had to retreat too. Old General Herkimer died from his wound and some families of the Valley were wiped out from the battle.

At first, it looked like both sides got it about the same. But when Colonel Gansevoort saw the ambush force leave, he sent Lieutenant Colonel Willet out on a raid of the Indians' camp. They burned most everything and took the rest. The Indians were mad and lots of them left right then and there. Then, once they heard that General Arnold was coming, they all took off and a few days later, the Brits and Tories ran off too, back to Canada."

"As well they might," said Caleb, and the other men murmured agreement. It was well known that Benedict Arnold stood out as the best General in the Continental Army. His men would do anything for him, and he was a "fighting general," not one to watch the battle from a safe place. Arnold liked to be right in the thick of things. All said he was a tough fighter. The Indians called him, "heap fighting chief" out of respect for his ferocity. For a white man to be admired by the fierce Iroquois warriors showed high praise. Arnold was back at Stillwater now and the scouts were hoping to fight under his command.

"Johnny," said Roland, "get me some of that busthead coffee and I'll read you boys about Bennington, another glorious victory."

Johnny poured some of the brown liquid into Roland's cup and Roland sipped at it without interest. The camp coffee wasn't great, but it was warm and soothed the throat.

"Here we go, boys, Bennington," said Roland and nodded at the faces filled with anticipation. They'd all heard the stories before, but hearing it read from off the latest handbill made them seem more real. Word of mouth always carried lots of rumors. You could hear everything from total defeat to Washington being crowned King.

"Well, as we all know, General Schuyler's "scorched earth" retreat made sure that there were no supplies around for the British to use. They have to ship everything along their supply line all the way from Canada. 'Course that takes a long time and along the way, our boys are always around to make it tough on them. After all the trouble he has getting to Fort Edward, Burgoyne realizes he's getting weaker, while we get stronger. He also hadn't reckoned on the fight we give him at Hubbarton and Fort Ann, neither."

The men nodded and smiled at the truth of it. General Schuyler's delay tactics had worked better than they could have hoped for. Burgoyne had taken too long to get to Fort Edward. By the time he got there, the Americans were long gone. First Schuyler had taken them south to Saratoga and then even further south to their present location at Stillwater. While the British were getting hungry and short of supplies, the American camp had been preparing. Between the reports of the gritty courage of American forces at Hubbarton, Fort Ann, Oriskany and Bennington, and outrage at the Jane McCrea incident, there seemed to be lots of men interested in being in on this scrap. There were now over 6,000 Continental soldiers at Stillwater and another 2,000 militia. It seemed like more men and supplies came rolling in every day.

"Well, Burgoyne's Tory scouts must have told him that over in Vermont we've got a lot of supplies. So, he sends out a force, a big one, maybe 800 men, made up mostly of Germans, to take Bennington. Old John Stark in New Hampshire has found out about this raid though, and he and Colonel Warner set out an ambush. On a hill along the Hoosick River, they fall on British and Germans. It goes back and forth for a while, but when Warner and his men get there it's all over. The few Brits and

The Ghosts of Saratoga · 55

Hessians that get away go back to Burgoyne, dragging their tails, whipped and with no supplies to show at all.

"So, boys, you can see what we got now. St. Leger's run back to Canada. That means Burgoyne won't get any help from the west. We've got men signing up daily, strong and ready to fight. General Gates has taken over from General Schuyler. That makes the New Englanders happy and they're joining us so fast the land can't hold us. The only thing we've got to worry about is General Washington holding back Howe in New York. And if General Washington can't hold 'em, then nobody can."

"So," said Caleb, "all we do is wait for Burgoyne to come to us. Or if he's smart, to run away back to Canada himself."

The men all murmured their approval of that idea and of the good battle reports. Roland rose, tossed his mess supplies over near his pack and walked a short distance up the hill. He stared off into the distance and after a few moments, Caleb joined him.

"I wish he would go back, Caleb. But he won't, will he?"

Caleb lit his pipe. "No, I reckon not, child. Too much at stake now."

"I don't want to make any more friends, Caleb. They just end up dead."

"Now lad," Caleb said. "I know the death of vanBrocklin hit you hard. But you can't keep away from good folks on the chance something bad'll happen to 'em. Bad things happen, Rollie, 'specially durin' war. Good people die, bad people die. But you have to live for today, as for tomorrow."

Roland turned to Caleb.

"You won't die, will you Caleb?" he asked.

The big man chuckled. "Ah now, lad, that's a claim no man can make."

"But you won't die here, now, will you?"

Caleb observed his young companion. He had forgotten Roland was still a boy. War made children grow up fast, this little one had already killed. But underneath, hid a youngster not yet eighteen. For all his courage and skill, he needed someone to tell him things would be all right. Caleb straightened and with deliberate slowness turned all the way around, puffing on the pipe. He shook his great, shaggy head.

"No child, no. I don't believe this is the place. Nor the time. I think there'll be a few more Christmas feasts for this old Irishman."

He clapped Roland on the shoulder.

"Come on, I think I hear Benny Moore workin' up his fiddle."

"O'Connor! McCaffrey! Grab your rifles!" came a shout.

The messmates stood and glanced around in alarm. Things were calm and secure in the camp. But young Captain Wilson came running toward them, all worked up. He stopped at their fire and stood, puffing, to catch his breath. Caleb, with his usual disregard for rank, grabbed Wilson's arm.

"What is it, boy? What's going on?" he asked.

"Morgan's riflemen... shooting contest...got to hurry, starting soon...main parade ground." Wilson paused and took a few deep breaths.

Caleb smiled. "I heard Colonel Morgan and his Virginia riflemen were here. A shooting contest, eh?"

"That's right," said Wilson, now under control," and the prize is a genuine Pennsylvania long rifle, one of the Old Waggoner's very own."

Roland's eyes grew wide. Colonel Daniel Morgan was maybe the most famous man in all the American forces. A scout and Indian fighter, he had fought for the British in the French War. While working as a wagon driver, a British officer struck him. Morgan, known for his strength and quick temper, knocked the man down. For this offense, he was whipped, five-hundred lashes. Some called it a miracle he had survived. It was no wonder he carried a nasty grudge against the British. Now he commanded a group of about three-hundred men, known as Morgan's Riflemen. The Riflemen were more feared by the British than any other group. They were the best shots in all North America. Every one of them could drop a man dead at three-hundred yards. The British called their rifles "Widow Makers."

Roland had a quality rifle himself. By the time he was ten, his father saw that Roland had a great eye and steady hand. He could hold his father's musket and outshoot every grown man around. On his son's fifteenth birthday, Evan McCaffrey had presented him with a used, but beautiful rifle. Peter vanBrocklin had picked it out himself. There was never any talk about how the gun had been paid for. But from that day, Roland had done the much-hated chores without complaint and the family always had meat on the table. Neighbors said they ate like the King. But a rifle owned by the greatest rifleman of them all...

Roland grabbed his rifle, pouch, and hat. He looked at Caleb.

"Not me, lad. This isn't a bunch of whiskey-brave blowhards, these boys are the best. You're the only one can even come close. Let's go."

At the parade ground, a huge crowd had gathered. The competitors were almost all Morgan's own men. They worshipped their Colonel and to own one of his weapons would be an honor. Here and there were a few men from other units. Roland knew a few of them, knew some others by reputation. He was far too nervous to notice, but many of them knew him too.

The targets were distant. With this group of shooters, only the most difficult shot could win. Dangling from a tree branch a good two-hundred-and-fifty yards away were several pieces of wood. Some clever artist had drawn pictures of King George on the wooden squares. Roland peered at the targets and whistled. He turned to Caleb.

"That's a fair shot, Caleb. As far as I've had to shoot in any contest."

"Nothing to it boy," Caleb chuckled, "Good luck!" He slapped Roland on the shoulder and walked away to join the crowd of onlookers.

"Listen up, marksmen!" a loud, deep voice bellowed. It was Morgan himself. He lived up to his legend, even in appearance. The rifleman was big, big as Caleb. He had on the most beautiful buckskin hunting shirt Roland had ever seen. His knee-length moccasins didn't even have holes in them.

"The idea is to shoot off old George's nose," said Morgan, and a wild cheer went up from the crowd. "Line up by height, men, and we'll shoot from tallest to shortest."

Roland's insides tightened. He saw he would be the shortest and have to go last. Roland was wiry and tough, but no one would ever call him big. His head came only to Caleb's shoulder. As the contestants moved around to get in place, Roland moved to the end of the line. There, a man who must have been one of Morgan's looked him up and down.

"Well son," said the man, "pears like we'll be last." He smiled broadly and held out his hand. "Wallace Travers, with Colonel Daniel Morgan's riflemen."

Roland shook his hand. The man's friendliness made him feel less nervous.

"Roland McCaffrey, with Colonel Andrew Colburn's scouts."

"Well young Roland McCaffrey, scout, the way I reckon it, we've got the lucky draw." said Travers.

"Really?" said Roland.

"Yep, we get to see who the competition is, all the mistakes that anybody can make, and we won't have to wait long for the second round."

"I guess you're right," said Roland, feeling the knots untie in his stomach.

The competition was strong. Roland couldn't believe how many men could hit such a small target at long range. But he too hit the mark and went to the next round. This time the targets were broken in half. A smaller King George was drawn on each half. Travers too went to the second round.

"See, Roland? Half these pretenders are out of our way already.

"Are you sure I'm not a pretender too?" asked Roland.

"No," said Travers, this time staring hard into Roland's eyes, "no, I think maybe you're the real thing, young McCaffrey. I have an instinct about these things."

Roland and Travers cleared the second round, along with ten other men. The third-round targets were the same size but before each shot, some men started them swinging back and forth. This caused the success rate to drop off and only four of the ten men before Travers hit the target. Before he stepped up to shoot,

Travers turned to Roland and winked.

"No challenge," he said, and true to his word, he blasted the swinging block.

Roland stepped up and loaded his rifle. He could feel the eyes on him. There was no way he could force himself to glimpse, but he knew Colonel Morgan would be watching him too. He nodded to the men at the target, who set it swinging. Roland sighed, held his breath, and squeezed the trigger. When the smoke cleared, the target still swung, undamaged.

"A miss!" called the man at the target.

A groan went up from the crowd. As he walked to join Caleb in the crowd a voice called out,

"Nice try Rollie!" Other voices joined in and by the time he reached Caleb, there was a great cheer going up for him. Roland turned bright red and scuffed his feet. Caleb jabbed him in the ribs with his elbow.

"These are your people child, tip your hat."

Still red, but now with a smile, he could no longer hold back, Roland stepped forward and lifted his battered hat to the crowd. He could feel his friends pounding his back as he tried to blend back in. Across the crowd, Roland saw a short, muscular man catch his eye and touch the brim of his hat. Even at this distance, Roland could sense the fire smoldering behind the man's dark eyes. He nodded in response and the man turned and moved to see the next round of shooting. Roland noticed he walked with a limp.

"Caleb, who is that man?"

"Where?" asked Caleb.

"Yonder," said Roland nodding his head in the man's direction, "the one with the limp."

Caleb laughed. "That man," he said, "is only the most famous general in this army and this war."

Roland stared after the man as he moved away. *So that is Benedict Arnold,* he thought.

The shooting contest continued. The eventual winner was one of Morgan's men, Tim Murphy. All the finalists were from the Riflemen. After the final, Travers came over to Roland.

"Well done McCaffrey, it's been a pleasure."

"Thanks," said Roland.

"Maybe next time we'll be shooting at redcoats together."

"I'd like that."

Travers nodded to Caleb and walked away.

"Wallace Travers," said Caleb.

"You know him?" asked Roland.

"I know of him," Caleb replied.

"He seems a good fellow."

"They say he may be the most dangerous man alive," said Caleb, watching the man walk away.

"What?" said Roland, surprised?

"They say he's got enough scalps to cover his walls. They say he'll kill a man for looking at him sideways." He poked at Roland, "They say he's a rough character lad. Be careful should you meet up with him again."

"He doesn't seem like a dangerous man," said Roland.

"Neither do you," said Caleb and he turned back to camp.

On the way back, Johnny Cooper came up to them.

"Sergeant, we're all supposed to report to Colonel Colburn at his tent."

"What for?" Caleb asked.

"Didn't say. Told me to let all the scouts know about it. He said to get there soon's you can."

Colonel Andrew Colburn sat waiting at his table until the scouts had assembled in the marquee. Roland was impressed with the size of the command tent. It must have been ten times the size of the tent he shared with his messmates. At last, an aide told Colburn that all the scouts were assembled. The Colonel stood, cleared his throat, and spoke in a loud, clear voice.

"Gentlemen, all signs point to Burgoyne continuing his invasion. There is no news of any action on Howe's part to move northward from New York, but our spies have information that the British plan is still to converge on and take, Albany. Thus, we are the only thing blocking the path from the north."

Colburn paused. Most of these men had served with him before. Even those new to his command knew of Colburn's reputation. He had risen through the ranks to become the head of scouts for the whole Northern Department. Yet he still often went out scouting himself, often working on his own and at night. His willingness to put himself at the same risks he asked of his men made him a popular leader. The men hung on his every word. He spoke again.

"I am very pleased," he said, and did smile a little," to inform you we have been placed under the command of General Arnold."

This brought a murmur of satisfaction. It was what most of the men were hoping for. Colburn had worked with Arnold before and knew him as a "fighting" officer. The General knew how to use his scouts; he didn't keep them sitting around idle.

"It is also my pleasure to tell you that Colonel Morgan's riflemen will also be part of the left wing working under General Arnold. They have already requested that we be available to assist them in the upcoming...ah...' festivities.' Obviously, this is high praise for our reputation. Your exact assignments will come soon, but I wanted you all to know what was going on as soon as I did. I'm sure you'll do us proud. That's all for now." Colonel Colburn nodded to his men and one of the Lieutenants shouted, "dismissed!"

Roland and Caleb were working their way out of the tent through the crowd when there was a tap on Roland's shoulder. He turned. It was one of Colburn's aides.

"McCaffrey?"

"Yes sir, Roland McCaffrey," said Roland and he took off his hat.

"Colonel would like to see you, McCaffrey." said the aide.

"Right now?" asked Roland.

"Right now," he replied.

Roland looked at Caleb, who shrugged and glanced toward the tent's exit to indicate he would wait outside. Roland followed the aide back to the Colonel's table. Colburn was once again sitting, puzzling over some maps. The aide bent down and whispered to Colburn, who nodded, continued to study the maps, and then waved an arm out to Roland.

"I'd ask you to sit down McCaffrey, but as you can see, I've only the one chair."

"That's all right sir, I'm a good stander. I'm fine." *Good stander?* thought Roland, *he must think me a perfect idiot.*

Colburn swept out his arm toward another man standing nearby.

"McCaffrey, this is Thaddeus Kosciuszko, who has come all the way from Poland to help us. He's in charge of our artillery and defense works."

Roland bowed a little to the man, unsure of Polish manners. "A pleasure, sir," he added.

"The pleasure is mine, young man," replied Kosciuszko in a thick accent.

"Mr. Kosciuszko believes this is a poor place for us to make a stand, McCaffrey," said Colburn. "I understand you know this area. We were wondering if you might have suggestions for a better site."

Roland stood speechless. He had not been expecting to be giving advice on battle strategy.

"Well, sir," he turned to Kosciuszko, "sirs," he added," I don't know that much about this sort of thing. Perhaps if you could tell what type of ground you'd be wanting."

"Ah yes, of course," said the Polish engineer, "how foolish of me, to think you know what I want. Here," he said and pointed to the map.

"This is British, about here, yes? This is us, you and me, here. I need place between to put guns to shoot..." he stood and made a downward motion with his hand, "to shoot..."

"Down?" suggested Colburn.

Kosciuszko pointed to Colburn. "Yes! I want to shoot down. To block from road and river. So, I seek maybe for place that is, is high and..." he struggled again for words and moved his two hands close together.

Roland saw the picture. "Narrow," he said. "I understand. You need someplace where you can see both the road and the river. You want to make a blockade and stop them."

Kosciuszko smiled and pointed at Roland, "Yes! It is so."

Roland never hesitated. "Well then, Colonel, I believe I may know the spot. "He stepped to the map. "Here, at a place called

Bemis Heights. Right near Neilson's place. The road comes right next to the river and there's steep hills on both sides. I know John Neilson. He could show you every inch of the whole area."

Colburn and Kosciuszko shrugged at each other. The Polish volunteer nodded.

"It sounds good, Colonel," he said to Colburn and turned to Roland. "I would like to see this place."

"So would I.," said a voice that came from the entrance to the tent. Colonel Colburn rose to his feet as Benedict Arnold strode across the marquee. He stopped beside Roland. The young scout felt his heart leap into his throat.

"You must take us there at once before Burgoyne finds it first."

At Bemis Heights, Kosciuszko charged his horse from spot to spot and scrambled up and down every cliff. Roland and John Neilson stood together smiling and watching the Polish volunteer. He was very excited.

"This spot, I think, Mr. Neilson. Water is nearby, yes?"

Neilson nodded.

"Right yonder, sir. Pure and cold, too."

"What do you think, General?" asked Colonel Hay, one of the officers sent to observe the area.

Roland noticed that Arnold usually was on horseback. When he dismounted, Arnold walked with a distinct limp. The longer he walked, the less noticeable his limp seemed, as if the leg had to loosen up. Roland knew the limp was from wounds Arnold received during the invasion of Canada. But despite the limp and his rather short stature, the General could move when he wanted to and always seemed to have his mind made up concerning where to go. Arnold nodded, pulled off his hat, and wiped the sweat off his face with his sleeve. He scowled for a moment at the scorching sun, then replaced his hat and looked over the terrain.

Roland watched him with awe. This was the man who led the first American victory of the war. He had taken Ticonderoga from the British, capturing the cannons Washington would use to drive the British fleet out of Boston. Arnold had marched on Quebec under brutal conditions and was wounded in a bitter defeat. He had almost single-handedly put together the American navy that met the British at Valcour Island. Some said he was too willing to risk the lives of his men. Others said Arnold should be in command of the Continental Army instead of George Washington. Even his enemies considered him one of the best military strategists on the continent.

"I like your choice Thaddeus," he said to Kosciuszko, "This hill would be the devil to storm, even with top troops. Your cannon can command both the Hudson and the road. Do you have an idea for rest of the fortification?"

"Yes, General, I do. We run our line from here to Mr. Neilson's house. Is ridge all the way. Once cannon in place, no way English can take you. No way."

Kosciuszko chuckled with delight and rubbed his hands together. A smile spread across his face as he walked over to Arnold. He patted the horse and grinned up.

"Is lovely ground, no? A good place to fight."

Arnold too smiled.

"That it is, Thaddeus, that it is. Mr. Neilson, what is this spot called again?"

"Well sir," replied Neilson, "This here spot is Bemis Heights. But these parts are called Saratoga."

Arnold repeated the name.

"Saratoga."

CHAPTER SEVEN - NEILSON'S FARM

The day of September 18, 1777, was fading into twilight. Most of the men had eaten and were finishing their coffee or tea. Officers were moving through the camp assigning the evening's guard duty. Roland could see up the hill to the "artillery park" where the ammunition was being stacked, counted and divided up once again. A group of men was gathering in a circle for a game of dice. To the east one of the fife and drum bands was playing, either for practice or entertainment. Whoever they were, they were good. Roland paused from cleaning up his plate and cup to listen for a moment. They were playing "Sailor's Hornpipe" and then without missing a beat moved right into "Soldier's Joy."

Roland picked up his plate and Caleb's. He headed to the stream to wash them. As he walked through the camp, he could hear music from all over. Somewhere a lone fiddler was bowing out "Red Haired Boy," and Roland thought of his family. This was one of his father's favorite tunes. In the past week, as it became clearer and clearer that the British were approaching, Roland had thought often of his family. He had written a letter to them and asked Caleb to deliver it if he was killed. This was a common practice among the men who could write. Roland had helped several other men with the writing of similar letters to wives, fathers, and children. No one wanted to think of their death, but they wanted their families to know that their last thoughts were of their loved ones. A tough infantryman had let a single tear roll down his cheek as he told Roland what he wanted written.

"This part's for Jacob." the soldier told Roland.

"Jacob, my dear and only son,

If you are hearing this read, it means I am dead. We ain't

never met but I want you to believe me when I say I loved you with all my heart. I had in mind that we'd spend many a day together. I'd teach you how to shoot and farm and maybe even how to fiddle. I always loved music, son. If'n you do learn, after all, maybe someday you'd play a verse of *Wind Shakes the Barley* in memory of me. Anyway, I have done been killed by a redcoat. When I come away to fight I never figgered on dyin', I want you to know that. But I've failed you, son. I'm sorry, so, so, sorry that I ain't there to hold you in my arms, to comfort you when you're sad, to see you grow to be a man. Wherever I am I'll always be your father and I'll try to watch over you the best I can."

At this point, the man turned away from Roland. Roland too had to wipe his eyes and nose. When the soldier turned back, Roland kept his eyes down, folded the paper and handed it to him.

"Thankee lad, I'm much obliged."

"It's a beautiful letter, sir. Let's hope no one ever reads it."

Roland strolled back to his tent. Along with the music and the sounds of men talking, he thought he could hear distant thunder. For a moment he considered if it might be cannon fire. He paused and closed his eyes, then turned into the light breeze and sniffed.

"Sniffing for your Sergeant?" Roland jumped; he hadn't noticed anyone nearby.

"No sir," Roland said, saluting Colonel Colburn, "I'm scenting for rain."

The Colonel tipped his head. "And?"

Roland leaned back his head and inhaled as if he were smelling a freshly baked pie.

"Yes sir, not that far away. Off to the northwest. Did you hear the thunder before?"

"Yes, at first I was afraid it might be cannon. Couldn't imagine who would be blasting at this time of day, or at what."

"I wondered the same thing, sir. That's why I was scenting, to smell for moisture on the breeze," explained Roland.

"That's a new one on me, McCaffrey. You're a true woodsman.

Any other weather signs?"

"Yes sir," he replied," right there."

Roland pointed out a group of crows flapping into the breeze.

"The birds?" asked Colburn.

"Aye, sir. Storm crows."

"Again, McCaffrey, that's a new one. Where did you learn your woodsmanship?"

"From a friend sir. Perhaps you know him, knew him, I mean. Captain Peter vanBrocklin?"

"I did know him, yes. A good man. I mourn his death."

"Me too, sir. I think about it every day."

"The war takes its toll, son. Liberty will have its pound of flesh."

"Sir?"

"Never mind, McCaffrey. Something from Shakespeare. But to business. I'm searching for Sergeant O'Connor; do you know where he is?"

"I do sir, right yonder with that group of men."

Colburn thanked him and strolled off to talk to Caleb. Roland watched him and noticed his quiet steps. The man seemed always to walk as if on eggshells. After a few minutes, he headed off, and Caleb rose and walked over to Roland.

"Things are happening, child. Make sure you're ready for action at a moment's notice," said Caleb.

"Why? What is it Caleb?" asked Roland.

"Well, for starters, we've been assigned to the Wagon Boy. If I know Morgan's men, they'll be wanting to reconnoiter the area before anything gets going. So, expect them to be calling. Second, Colonel's going out right now to the British position. On his own. I'm to report him missing if he's not back by dawn. That's not a message I'd care to give to General Arnold."

Caleb rubbed his hairy knuckles along the side of his face. Roland was surprised to see that the Sergeant had taken advantage of the break in action to shave. Without the red stubble, it was easier to notice the white scar running from his nose to under his ear. Roland had wondered before how he got the scar, but it didn't seem proper to ask.

"Is this it, Caleb? Are they coming?" Roland asked.

"Looks like it, lad." Caleb rested the giant hand on Roland's shoulder. "Listen, get our gear together. We'll sling a tarp tonight and sleep out. I don't like the sound of things, don't want to get surprised. Move our things up to that grove of maples by the Fort. I've a mind to talk to Whitcomb, see what he knows. Then I've got to stop by the hospital."

"The hospital? Is something wrong?" asked Roland.

"Nah, nothing's wrong, child. Just move the gear, eh?"

Roland's heart was racing as he moved to follow Caleb's instructions. Caleb must be expecting a nighttime maneuver, always a dangerous mission. The "fort" Caleb referred to was a barn owned by Neilson. General Gates had ordered the barn fortified and it was being used as a headquarters. It sat at the top of a ridge that led down to the river. Roland could see a great deal of activity at the fort. Men were going in, going out, giving instructions to other men who ran off and returned. Roland was organizing the equipment, wondering why Caleb was going to the hospital and trying to keep an eye on the fort. From the corner of his eye, he saw a man point to him. Another soldier came running up toward Roland.

"Are you Roland Mc Caffrey of Colburn's scouts?"

"I am," replied Roland, now at full alert.

"I have instructions for you to report to Colonel Morgan's tent at once."

"Should I bring my rifle and...and...pack?" stammered Roland.

The man had a very serious expression on his face. "Yes, I have the impression that would be wise.

Roland scribbled a short note of explanation to Caleb. He knew Caleb couldn't read it but hoped he would recognize it as relevant and ask someone to read it to him.

Then he raced off to Colonel Morgan's tent. He announced himself to a Corporal and was told to go right in.

Morgan was standing and, as always, dressed in his buckskins. He was ready for action. Having spent time around Caleb, Roland was used to large men, but Morgan loomed legendary, and Roland couldn't keep himself from shivering. Morgan was giving some instructions to one of his men and nodded at

Roland. In a moment the man bolted out of the tent. Morgan walked over to Roland.

"McCaffrey, I've got a small problem and I need you to scout for a group of my men."

"Sir," said Roland.

"It's like this. Warren's Massachusetts militiamen, you know what they're like," Morgan raised his eyebrows and nodded to Roland, who, in reality, knew nothing about either Warren or Massachusetts," Well, they've got it into their heads to do some reconnaissance this evening. That's fine, I don't want to stop any man with the guts to take some initiative. But, they're my responsibility and I don't want them to get into something they can't handle. I want you to shadow them and if something comes up, get back to me quick as a rabbit. You understand?"

"Yes sir," replied Roland, "but..."

"What is it, son?" asked Morgan.

"Do I need to let anyone else know what I'm doing sir?"

"I've requested that you be assigned to my unit for this engagement. Keep Colburn advised, but you're under my command."

Roland couldn't help but blush. *Me, requested by the most famous fighting group in the army.*

"It's an honor, sir." he managed to choke out.

"It's war son," replied Morgan. "On your way."

Roland saluted and slipped out of the tent. First, he had to find the Massachusetts boys if he was going to follow them. He ran the local terrain through his mind and guessed that they would follow the slope to the Great Ravine. That was the area where scouts had last seen British troops.

Roland realized he had seen John Neilson at a campfire nearby. His knowledge of the area could be most helpful. He ran off through the gathering dark.

Roland and Neilson weaved through the woods. To save time Neilson had suggested a direct route rather than staying on trails. In the fading light, it would be a tricky maneuver. Roland let John lead the way. It was easy to pick up the militia's trail.

The snapped branches and crushed vegetation left evidence of their passing.

A short while later they came on Warren's men. The militiamen didn't know the area and hadn't requested a scout. They were making slow progress. It wasn't a large group and they had fanned out to cover a wider area. As he watched, Roland saw another man come running to the center of the group and jabber with excitement. One of them whistled several times and the whole bunch regrouped and headed off to the west. Roland followed them while Neilson circled off to the side.

The woods opened onto a small field where a farmer, maybe Mr. Freeman, had planted potatoes. Freeman himself was a Loyalist who had taken his family and joined the British when the American army came into the area. Roland could see several men in the field digging. Even in the poor light, he could recognize the uniforms of the British army. There figured to be twenty-five or thirty of them. Roland looked for Indian scouts or British sentries and saw none. These men must have taken it upon themselves to find some food. That would be a useful piece of information for Colonel Morgan.

Warren's men had spread out, encircling the edge of the field. Without warning, they opened fire on the British. At least a dozen men dropped on the spot, dead or wounded. Others ran off like jackrabbits while a few grabbed their muskets and tried to return fire. The Massachusetts men were positioned in the trees and at this close range, even a musket was accurate. It took only a few minutes before any British soldier left standing had run off. With a whoop, the militiamen were in pursuit, with Roland following.

The chase lasted only a few moments until the militiamen realized they had gotten turned around in the excitement and were now altogether lost. The sun long down, twilight was turning to dark. Roland could hear nervous voices from all directions. He knew what had to be done.

"Massachusetts militia! Can you hear me?"

There was a jumble of surprised voices followed by a louder barking of what must have been an officer.

"You men, quiet! I can't hear!" he shouted. Roland could hear the fear and anger in his voice. He saw the man turn in circles, trying to figure out where Roland's voice had come from.

In these conditions, Roland was willing to wait; he didn't want one of the excited militiamen to shoot him thinking it was a British trick.

"This is Sergeant Edward Hanover! Who calls to us?" the man shouted.

"Roland McCaffrey, of Colonel Colburn's scouts and Mr. John Neilson."

A crunching of twigs startled him, and Roland whirled around, expecting to be facing an entire force of British soldiers. To his relief, it was only Neilson. The man was a farmer and had a farmer's step, not a scout's. He seemed upset.

"Bloody fools near shot me," he snarled.

"Thank God," called the Sergeant. "Where are you and can you show us the way to the camp?"

Roland stood clear of the tree he had been using for cover.

"This way. Are you all here?"

"There's no way to tell. We didn't run roll call. Truth to tell, we didn't expect action." said Hanover.

Roland walked over to the group of men.

"Then take the men you have here Sergeant, if you will, and head back with Mr. Neilson here. I'll sweep the area to make sure no one's left behind."

"My thanks, McCaffrey. I'm not of a mind to stay out here long. If them British was here, the rest can't be far."

"I'm of the same notion, Sergeant." said Roland, "I won't be long."

His sweep turned up three more of the Massachusetts men and before long they were all back at the American camp. Sergeant Hanover raced off to tell Colonel Warren news of their rout of the British. Roland reported to Colonel Morgan.

From his vantage point high in a tree, Colonel Colburn watched the British coming. First, off the highlands, they had occupied for a few days, and then into and across the Great Ravine. It was a large force; Colburn estimated the number at over

5,000 up to 6,000 men and several dozen cannon. Somewhere in that mass of men, Colburn knew, was "Gentleman" Johnny Burgoyne, the man who considered the Continental army little more than rabble.

"Well, Johnny," hissed Colburn, "we'll soon see who's rabble and who's a man."

Colburn took one last look around him in the fading light. He heard the low cawing of a crow nearby. A small smile played across his face and he turned into the breeze and sniffed. Then chuckling to himself, he climbed down and headed back to camp.

Inside Fort Neilson, Colonel Warren was busy reporting the news of his men's victory to General Gates.

"My boys caught 'em by surprise General. Took most of 'em down and sent the rest packing."

"Yes, that's good Colonel," replied Gates. "Still, I wish you had seen fit to advise me of your action. Keep in mind in the future that I expect all my officers to clear orders through me."

Warren's eyes narrowed at this scolding, but he said nothing.

"What would you say the enemy's numbers are like?" asked Gates.

"Considering how bold they were to be out digging up potatoes, I'd say too many to wrangle with General."

"General Gates," said Benedict Arnold, "I urge you to take action. There is unfortified high ground to our west. If Burgoyne's scouting parties discover it, we could find ourselves flanked by morning. Let me move in force now. We can take the initiative and dictate the action."

Horatio Gates glowered around the room at his officers. He was a cautious man. His scouting reports had him outnumbering the enemy by over a thousand men. Supplies had been coming in daily from Albany for weeks. Kosciuszko had the defenses in place. The American army held the high ground. He could afford to outwait Burgoyne. British supplies and men grew less with each passing day. Perhaps if he waited long enough, Burgoyne would turn around and go back to Ticonderoga or even to Canada. Gates would receive cheers for stopping the British invasion and there would be little risk.

Gates' gaze rested on the agitated Arnold. *The man is rash,* thought Gates, *but what if he's right? What if they **do** flank us? Then I might go down in history as the man who handed over the nation to the British.* Gates could feel his stomach churn and his mouth turn dry. He reached for his mug and took a long drink of ale. He nodded his head, hoping it made him look wise, and again looked at each of his officers.

"It is my belief we still have the night to consider our options. Burgoyne would be foolish to try a large troop movement at night in unfamiliar territory. We have the advantage of numbers and good ground. I suggest we all get a good night's rest and, on the morrow, we shall decide on our action."

Arnold was about to protest when Colburn burst through the door.

"General Gates," said Colburn, "the crisis is near."

CHAPTER EIGHT - FREEMAN'S FARM PART I

The morning of September 19, 1777, broke gray with a drizzling rain and thick fog. Roland could only see ghostly outlines across camp as he packed his gear and readied for battle. The damp night had chilled him, and he shivered as he worked. Colonel Colburn's report left little doubt that the British would, had to, advance. General Gates was not one to make rash decisions. He would enter into a fight as a last resort. Still, he was afraid it would be the way soon enough.

Roland and some of the other scouts tried to warm themselves beside a smoky fire. A young Continental came by and told them a mighty battle was raging right inside the General's headquarters. General Arnold was arguing for action. He wanted to send out flanking maneuvers in force. His position called to make the first move, on the ground of his choosing, before the British could move all their forces into position. Gates, ever cautious, wanted to wait and see what Burgoyne would do. His position was the Americans had numbers, supplies and time on their side. If they could hold long enough, General Washington might send more troops up the Hudson to help them. The debate had gotten hot.

The men at the fire voiced their opinions, some backing each idea. Roland remained silent as he munched a piece of bread with honey. His instincts believed in action and Arnold's plan, but that meant more death. The image of Peter vanBrocklin's broken body forced itself into his brain. Death seemed to play a large part in his life anymore. He wasn't sure how he felt about that. As he mulled over his thoughts, Caleb came up to the group.

"Well, children," he said," we, at least, are going out."

Roland stirred from his thoughts.

The Ghosts of Saratoga· 75

"Sergeant?" he said.

"That's right, lad. While the generals argue over who does what, we're supposed to keep an eye on the Brits. Then let the bigwigs decide what's to do."

Caleb looked around the group. They were all waiting for him to say more.

"That's it, boys. You know where they are, try not to get killed."

They broke up to get their packs and go. Caleb called out.

"Oh, and I know all our reports say their Indians are gone but I'd be careful just the same."

A few minutes later Roland and Caleb were heading off to the northwest. It was still too early to expect any movement from the British, but they wanted to get an idea of their position as soon as possible. That way they could follow any actions.

"Well, this weather means one thing good, lad," said Caleb.

"It does?" replied Roland, "I can't imagine what."

Caleb raised his rifle. "It means we won't be shot."

Roland laughed as he realized what Caleb meant. In this rain, the powder would never flash. Any fighting today would have to wait until the sun-dried things out.

The weather was already improving when they saw first sign of the British army. Despite Caleb's warning, it did look like the Indian scouts had abandoned the British. The scouts crept close to the British lines without any sign of scouts. Selecting a spot that offered cover and seemed to promise some warming morning sun, they settled in and ate some biscuits. Caleb rechecked their supplies and Roland took out his spyglass.

When 8:00 came General Burgoyne could wait no longer. The thick fog remained, and the rain hadn't yet stopped. But his weather experts predicted the day would turn suitable for battle. He had laid out his plan last night. His officers were ready. General Fraser was considered the best officer on the continent, Hamilton was capable and, though he hated to admit it, the German vonRiedesel was not only tough as nails but resourceful and a good tactician. Burgoyne would accompany Hamilton's troops.

The plan was so simple, that Burgoyne believed even "Granny" Gates would figure it out before long. The real problems could come if Arnold saw his strategy and reacted before the British forces were all in position.

Burgoyne sent his men out in three groups. VonRiedesel would move down the river road in a southerly direction. Although he had a part in the battle plans, his main responsibility was to protect the supplies and boats. Hamilton would be the British center and would cross the ravine to the open ground near Freeman's farm. Fraser would be the right wing and was the key to the plan. The Americans had left the high ground to their left (the west) unfortified and unoccupied. If Fraser's men, with cannon, could take that high ground their guns could fire down into the rebel's main position and drive them back. At that point, Hamilton would advance and push them toward the river, where the German would be waiting. If everything fell together, he could force a surrender today. At worst he would push Gates's army further south.

Even if things didn't fall together, Burgoyne had little choice. Rebel attacks on his supply line to Ticonderoga had made it close to impossible to get food or ammunition to this area. St. Leger had long since retreated, along with most of the Indians Burgoyne had counted on for scouts. In recent days, Burgoyne's intelligence reports had gotten so poor that the raid on a foraging party was his first solid clue of the closeness of the American position. He still didn't have information on the size of the American force. He knew, however, that the enemy's numbers were growing every day even as his shrank. Between desertion and disease, his force would soon be inadequate to take Albany, even if he could keep to the timeline. It was also obvious that any help from Howe would not be soon in arriving. The time had to be now.

Back at Fort Neilson, Gates was receiving a constant flow of information from his scouts. As they reported the movement of the three British wings, General Arnold became more and more agitated. When Roland arrived to tell them that Fraser's grenadiers were moving westerly, Arnold could stand it no longer and stomped over to Gates' table.

"General Gates, I beg you! Do you not see their strategy? Fraser plans to take the high ground on our left. I can assure you he will have artillery with him. If he holds that position, we will be at his mercy!" Arnold's face shone red with emotion and his fists were clenched. He shook, struggling to contain himself. Colonel Morgan paced in the corner. It was obvious he shared Arnold's opinion. The other officers were watching the battle of wills between Gates and Arnold. Nervous, Roland shifted his weight from foot to foot. He wasn't sure he should still be there, but no one had dismissed him. Gates sighed.

"General Arnold, calm yourself. It is not yet noon. We have plenty of time to decide on our strategy."

Arnold huffed away and kicked savagely at something only he seemed to see on the floor. Gates turned to the Polish engineer Kosciuszko, whose judgment he had learned to trust.

"Thaddeus?" asked Gates.

"I must agree with General Arnold, sir. Is more than possible to put cannon on the western hill. From there, we make easy targets."

"Yes! You see?" cried Arnold, striding back across the room, "If we let Burgoyne choose the time and place, he will have us on open ground where he can use his artillery and bayonets. Let us take advantage of this thick forest. It's the perfect ground for skirmishing with light infantry and rifles. PLEASE General, let me act!"

Gates considered his options. He went over the latest report. It indicated the British were indeed following the plan described by Arnold.

"All right General," said Gates, "you may take Morgan and Dearborn out to see what they are up to. If necessary, you may engage. But you are to commit only your wing to any action."

"Thank you, sir," beamed Arnold, and he saluted and turned to go.

"General Arnold!" called Gates.

Arnold stopped and turned, worried that Gates had already

changed his mind.

"Remember old friend," said Gates, now standing, "I am in command here."

Arnold turned away and hurried off, followed by Morgan, who was giving Roland instructions for an approach to the British positions.

General Arnold wanted as clear a picture of the British layout as possible. He accompanied Morgan's riflemen, with Roland scouting. They maneuvered toward the British center. Dearborn's infantry was to follow close behind and spread out to the west to block the advance of Fraser's corps.

It was a little after noon when Roland brought them to a spot where there was a clear view of the open courtyard around Freeman's farm. There appeared to be a large advance party of Indians moving in the area. Arnold scowled at them for a few moments and turned to his old fighting companion.

"Colonel Morgan, you and I have seen too many redskins to be deceived by that garb of paint and feathers; they are asses in lion's skins, Canadians and Tories. Let your riflemen cure them of their borrowed plumes."

Roland stared into the clearing. General Arnold was right, these weren't Indian scouts at all. A group of white men had dressed up to fool them. They didn't realize the Americans were near. The advance party was strolling along, enjoying the sun that had broken through and eating hard biscuits.

Morgan grabbed him by the shoulder.

"Come on, let's get my men in position. Is there a way we can circle that clearing and still keep out of sight?"

"Yes," replied Roland, "there's even a footpath that will take us around."

Before they headed out, Morgan gave his last-minute instructions.

"Remember men, concentrate your fire on officers and artillerymen. Even in the smoke, you can see the red sash of the officers. It won't always be a killing shot, but it'll take them down. And in case any of you wooden-heads can't figure it out, the artillerymen are the ones standing next to the cannon."

A chuckle ran through the group and Morgan turned to Roland.

"Lead on, McCaffrey."

The riflemen were experienced woodsmen. With Roland's advice, they moved into positions around the clearing of Freeman's farm. The surrounding forest was dense and offered good cover. The Americans moved into accurate rifle range without the British knowing they were there. Along with the rest of the unit, Roland readied his rifle and selected his target. He sighted in on a man who was giving instructions to two others, figuring he must be an officer.

I'm sorry, but you shouldn't be here. You should be with your family in England. How I hate you for being another death on my conscience.

A pistol fired the signal. Almost as one, dozens of rifles blasted the British in the clearing. The riflemen's' aim was lethal. Every officer dropped dead or wounded along with most of the regulars. Despite Morgan's shouts to hold their positions, the results of this initial volley had the men's blood up and with a wild whoop, they charged to finish the British.

Caught up in the excitement, Roland charged with them. It was a crazed, unorganized attack, men running helter-skelter, some waving tomahawks, some swinging their rifles as clubs, some trying to shoot the retreating British as they ran. Roland had lost all sense of caution. He ran after a group of fleeing redcoats. As they broke into a small area of shrubs, he fired and one of them crashed headlong into a tree. From his left, another rifle shot rang out and a second British soldier jerked to a stop. The man dropped his musket and twisted around. As he did, his head seemed to explode as another rifle ball killed him.

The horror of the violence seemed to bring Roland back to reality. Despite himself, he walked up and stared down at the dead soldiers, his rifle still not reloaded. His stomach churned, and he was gagging when one of Morgan's men came running along and slapped him on the back.

"Come on, we've got them on the run, "he shouted and disappeared into the forest.

Roland realized that it was Wallace Travers, from the shooting contest. With a last glance at the destroyed men at his feet, Roland raced off after him. As he caught up to Travers, Roland heard loud shouting, followed a few seconds later by the unmistakable sound of volleys of musket fire. In seconds the woods were filled with flying musket balls. One smashed into a tree near Roland's head and Travers yanked him off his feet onto the ground.

"What the hell is going on?" growled Travers.

Before Roland could answer, they heard shouting and the sounds of men running through the woods. Now the woods around them were filled with Morgan's men, running in full retreat. Travers grabbed one as he raced by.

"What's going on?" he shouted.

"It's the British center, Wallace. We've charged right into the front ranks." The man tore away from Travers and raced off at top speed. Travers pulled Roland to his feet.

"Well, young McCaffrey. If you've the belly for it, I reckon we can get off one more round before they get to us with their bayonets."

"I'm with you". said Roland, though his throat was tight. He reloaded.

There wasn't long to wait. The sound of footsteps signaled the approach of the British front rank. Then he could see them. Even in the thick woods, they were marching shoulder to shoulder, step by step, with their bayonets fixed, ready to pierce him to the heart. He and Travers were still hidden by the underbrush. They would have a clear shot.

"Ready?" he heard Travers whisper.

"Yes." It was all he could say. The advancing enemy moved close. He could see into the second and third ranks. He knew as soon as he fired, the second rank would step forward and blast the woods with musket fire.

"All right then," said Travers, "when they pass that hemlock, you take that fat one in the middle. Then run like the devil himself is on your tail."

Roland tried to reply, but his mouth was dry and all he could do was nod. He forced his body to relax. He leaned against a tree to help steady himself. The rifle felt smooth and cool and familiar in his hands. The weight, the smell of the powder in the pan, these were old friends.

He took in a breath, held it and centered his aim on the fat soldier's body. When the man passed the tree, Roland fired. He knew he had to run, but watched long enough to see the man crumple, fall to the ground, and trip the man next to him. Then Roland sprang to his feet and raced after Travers through the thickest woods they could see. The crackle of muskets split the air and moments later he could hear the cruel musket balls tearing through the late summer leaves all around him. One glanced off his shoulder and Roland ran for dear life from the one with his name on it. He couldn't help himself and shot a glance over his shoulder to check the pursuit. When he turned back, he smashed into a tree and fell back flat on his backside.

At least he had thought it was a tree. But as he shook off the impact and sat up, he saw a man. A man in the uniform of the Continental army! The man smiled and helped Roland to his feet.

"Easy there, youngster. Nothing to worry on. It's Major Dearborn's infantry here to clean up this mess you started."

Looking around, Roland could see the woods full of infantrymen. It must be a counter-charge, the men had bayonets fixed. The man gestured with his head for Roland to continue on past. It took Roland a few minutes to get through the ranks and by the time he was through, the sounds of pitched battle began again. Dearborn's men were exchanging fire with the British. In a few minutes, the air filled with smoke and the firing let up. A voice ordered a charge. The infantry roared and attacked.

Without a bayonet there wasn't much Roland could do but watch. Dearborn's men must have gotten the upper hand for soon the battle moved out of sight. Roland realized he couldn't see any of Morgan's men. While he was trying to find them, he heard a faint turkey call.

How odd, he thought, *a turkey calling in the middle of a battle.*

The turkey called again, and Roland saw some movement in

the woods. He crouched down, reaching for the loaded pistol tucked into his waist. But it was one of Morgan's men. Another appeared, as if out of nowhere. They moved toward the turkey call. Roland followed.

Soon the wood filled with riflemen. Roland could see Morgan. The head rifleman was using a slate and a corn cob to make the turkey call sounds. He was using it to draw his men back, to reorganize. Roland saw Caleb in the gathering and moved to join him.

"Are you unhurt then, child?" asked the Irishman.

"A musket ball hit my shoulder," said Roland. He had forgotten to check it until now. "but it bounced off. Doesn't even seem to have ripped my shirt."

Caleb rested his heavy hand on Roland's shoulder.

"Gonna be a hot one today lad, and I don't mean the weather. I can't be watchin' to wipe your nose, so you be careful eh?"

Roland smiled and nodded. He realized with a twinge of guilt he hadn't asked Caleb how he fared. He was about to speak when Morgan's voice boomed over the group.

"The infantry has engaged the British center. I want you to fan out to the edges in both directions and concentrate fire on the flanks. Is that..."

Morgan stopped his instructions as a huge black horse skittered to a stop beside them. General Arnold had arrived on the scene.

CHAPTER NINE - FREEMAN'S FARM PART II

"There's been a change," said Arnold, still astride his black charger. "We will hit between the British center and their right. Fraser's still after the high ground and he's opened a gap. If we can get through, we'll be right on Johnny's backside and the day is won."

Morgan moved closer to Arnold, resting his hand on the horse's side.

"But won't we be leaving our flank open to Fraser? The high ground?"

"It can't be helped," replied Arnold. "Hit them hard and fast. That will force them to recall Fraser to help. I've already called up reinforcements, as I intend to assault their center presently."

Colonel Colburn rode up on a glum gray horse. He gave a sloppy salute to Arnold and nodded to Morgan.

"General Arnold, sir," said Colburn, "I must inform you that General Fraser has begun his flanking maneuver in earnest. Unless we act now, he'll hold the high ground within the hour."

Arnold pulled off his hat and beat it against his leg several times. His horse flinched with each strike but held steady.

"Damn, damn, damn," cursed the general.

"Dan," he said to Morgan, "you've got to hold Fraser. If he flanks us, all is lost. Don't despair, I'll be back." And with that, he kicked his horse into action, and they charged off, splattering clods of dirt behind.

Morgan turned around and saw Caleb.

"O' Connor! Report!" he cried.

Caleb trotted over to Morgan. Roland went with him.

"We've got to move fast," the Colonel said to the scouts, "Take us the fastest route to the west. We'll deploy to that high ground from here."

Roland and Caleb led the riflemen off to the west. Morgan soon realized he didn't have enough men. They were spread far too thin. Without the infantry to back them up, his riflemen could never hold off a bayonet charge. If they couldn't keep the British at bay, they'd be in trouble. At last, they had the distance covered, although there were huge gaps in their line.

They didn't have long to wait. The advance troops of Fraser's force were soon in sight. Morgan's orders were to fire at will at the leading edge. Knowing they would need all the time they could get; the riflemen fired at the absolute limit of their range. Even spread as thin as they were, the accuracy of the riflemen cut down man after man in the front rank of the advance. At first, the holes were filled from behind as fast as a man went down. But as the British got closer the marksmen became even more effective and the advance faltered. Morgan knew the riflemen were outnumbered. Soon the British would be in melee range. The only alternative was retreat.

The Colonel was discussing the best withdrawal route with Caleb when General Arnold again appeared on his black stallion. And with him, reinforcements!

As ranks of Continental army soldiers filled into the lines, the beat of the British drums changed, and they halted. Soon it became a staring match as British and Americans formed their lines, out of each other's musket range. Morgan ordered his riflemen to keep up the fire, and after a few officers fell dead, the British line retreated and reformed. The action settled down. Arnold again charged over to Morgan.

"Colonel, I want your men to regroup. Take to the woods and maneuver towards the British center. I still aim to hit that gap before this day is over."

Before Morgan could even answer, Arnold was gone again. Morgan scowled after him.

"I wish he could take one damn minute to talk through things," he growled. "Well, O'Connor," he said to Caleb, "You heard the man, let's get 'em going."

The riflemen vanished into the woods at the same time as Dearborn's infantry arrived at the scene. Roland raced through the woods, his heart beating like claps of thunder. From the east, he could hear musket fire. That meant that another part of the American army had engaged the British center. It didn't sound like it was a full-fledged battle yet, more like scattered skirmishes.

Along with the distant sounds of gunfire, Roland picked up another sound that didn't belong in the woods. He stopped, tried to catch his breath and clear the roaring of his blood pumping. It was faint, but there. The sound of many feet moving through the woods. They were quiet, sneaking steps, but there were too many to keep the sound down. Roland turned, caught the eye of the man next in line behind him and pointed to his ear. The man turned and held his arm high. Without a sound, he scurried up to Roland.

"What have you got McCaffrey?" he whispered.

"Footsteps, a lot of them. Must be part of Fraser's men."

"Where, do you think?" asked another voice. It was Wallace Travers; he commanded this group of riflemen. The man always seemed to appear out of thin air.

Roland listened, gave a thin smile and whispered back at Travers.

"Between us and Dearborn. We've got them flanked."

"Very good," Travers patted Roland's arm. "We'll move on my command."

Roland nodded. Travers moved away without even a rustle. Roland was impressed by his stealth, the man moved like an Indian. Roland loaded his rifle and pistol and waited for Travers' signal to advance.

The sounds of battle had stopped off to the east. Somewhere to the west loomed General Fraser's force, the elite corps of the British army. They were hard men, experienced and tough. This would be a dangerous engagement. Roland wondered where Caleb had got to. But the whistle of Travers' signal broke through his thoughts and he crouched through the thick woods.

It wasn't long before the British were in sight. It was Fraser's Grenadiers all right, he could see the tall bearskin hats moving in the woods. If not for the seriousness of the situation it was almost laughable. The British were moving in force through the woods, trying to sneak as best they could. They were wearing red uniforms and tall hats. They stood out like sore thumbs. And not a scout around. They hadn't a clue that Morgan's riflemen, the best marksmen alive, were at this moment taking aim at them.

Roland tried to find an officer but couldn't, so he sighted in on the tallest Grenadier he could find. As the man tried to sneak along, Roland followed him with the barrel of his rifle. He was waiting for Travers' shot, the signal to open fire. It roared out, off to Roland's right. Roland's target froze, then crouched down. Roland shot. It wasn't a good shot, crashing into the man's shoulder. He dropped his musket and grasped his wounded arm. As Roland reloaded, he decided that even though it wasn't a killing shot, he'd put the man out of action for now and he searched for another target.

The woods had now erupted with the sound of rifle fire. The British were responding with their muskets, but the riflemen were well hidden in the dense vegetation. They were working outside musket range anyway, and the British seemed to have few riflemen with them. Roland could hear officers shouting, trying to organize the ranks, and he scanned the woods trying to find one. Before he could get off another shot, a loud war whoop came from his right.

He could see Dearborn's infantry, charging headlong into the British. Taking advantage of the chaos caused by the riflemen, Arnold had chosen this moment to charge the British flank. There was scattered musket fire, but it wasn't long before the fight turned into hand to hand combat. Roland moved forward, trying to find a position where he could see what was happening. The woods were swarming with men, some thrusting bayonets at each other, some swinging muskets as clubs, others fighting with tomahawks, knives or even their hands. In the mad tangle, there was no way to get off a shot without knowing whether it would hit friend or foe.

Frustrated, Roland zigzagged through the battle, hunting for a position where he could see who was where. In tight battle conditions like this, there wouldn't be time to aim. He pulled his pistol. It wasn't very accurate, but he knew he couldn't tangle with a British Grenadier in a hand to hand fight.

The Ghosts of Saratoga· 87

To his right, a Continental soldier flew through the air and landed not ten feet from him. The man hit the ground with a grunt, his musket falling away. A redcoat leaped from the woods; bayonet poised. The Continental's eyes grew wide and he tried to roll out of the way as the Grenadier stabbed for his heart. He was partly successful, the blade missed his heart but pierced through his side below his ribs, pinning him to the ground. He let out a high cry as the Grenadier yanked his bayonet out and reared back to run him through again.

The Englishman caught the movement out of the corner of his eye as Roland raised his pistol. For an instant, their eyes locked. Roland fired. Even with a pistol, this was point blank range. The British soldier fell back as if he had been kicked by a horse. Roland raced to the injured infantryman's side.

"How bad are you hurt; can you talk?" he asked.

The man sat up and reached a hand inside his shirt, on which the blood was already soaking through.

"I think I'll be all right, thanks to you, friend. Hmm, a little hole." He pulled his hand out, glistening with blood.

Roland cringed, "We've got to get you back to camp!"

The man grabbed his arm. "No reason to panic, son. I've been stabbed before and worse than this." He nodded his head at the grenadier. "Get his shirt and help me bind the wound, I'm not done for the day yet. The fightin's still on, you know."

It was true, although the sounds of the fight had moved away toward the north. Roland walked over to the dead Englishman. He had killed him sure enough, and by intention, but he hadn't planned on picking over the dead body. He hesitated, looked back at the tough infantryman hunched over, holding his side, and then pulled off the Grenadier's coat.

The infantryman proved as tough as his talk. Roland helped him tear up the Grenadier's shirt and coat into bandages and bind the wound. Then he helped him to his feet. By the time the man had his musket back in his hands, the color was returning to his face. He smiled at Roland.

"I'll not delay you longer, son. But as you've saved my life, I'd care to know your name to tell my wife and children who the angels sent."

"My name's Roland McCaffrey but I don't think my deeds this day will stand me well with angels."

The man laughed and shook Roland's hand.

Roland followed the gunfire. It was slowing down. By the time he came to a clearing, it had almost stopped. The Americans were in force among the trees at the edge. The British troops were massing in the clearing, dressing their units into position. Roland scanned the scene for someone he knew.

He could see a mix of Morgan's riflemen and Dearborn's infantry. Also, infantry from another group Roland didn't know. The woods provided good cover and as he moved along Roland noticed that every few minutes a rifleman would shoot into the clearing. Each time, another British soldier would fall. They couldn't get out of range but weren't yet organized enough to mount a charge. So, Morgan was having his men use them for target practice.

Roland's spirits rose as he saw Caleb sitting against a tree, smoking a pipe.

"Caleb!" he shouted.

"Ah, lad! Good to see you alive! Have a seat."

"What's going on Caleb? Why are we just sitting here? Why are they just sitting there letting us shoot at them? Why?"

Caleb chuckled. "It's a peculiar situation, I agree. It's like this: We hit them hard with that charge. So hard I think maybe it was a lesson them Grenadiers won't forget. But I've got to give them Brits their due, they're tough as the day is long. We had them flanked and outnumbered but Dearborn couldn't break through. And his boys being rough men themselves."

"But why are we here? At this clearing?" Roland was still trying to get everything sorted out.

"Well child, old Fraser got his men into that clearing and darn if they didn't dress the ranks again. Even got some field cannon set up. Volley fire in the open is their style fight. If we charge across that open ground, they'll harrow us down like wheat."

"Then why are they sitting there, giving us targets?"

"I can't tell that for sure. My guess is they've got orders to take the western high ground. Fraser won't withdraw without Burgoyne's say-so and they don't dare move into the woods

The Ghosts of Saratoga· 89

again because they know we're here."

Roland shook his head. "It still doesn't make any sense to me Caleb."

"Nor me, child. Still, officers aren't like regular men. Their minds work in a funny way." He waved his pipe in the air. "Like they're dropped on their head or something."

"Thank you, Sergeant O'Connor, that's high praise coming from you."

It was Colonel Morgan himself., He'd come upon them unnoticed.

Roland jumped to his feet. Caleb remained sitting. Roland was stunned; it seemed no one made much of an impression on Caleb. And officers always seemed to let him off.

"Beggin' the Colonel's pardon, sir. Present company excepted."

Morgan laughed. "No offense taken, Sergeant. I've expressed similar views on officers myself, as you well know."

Caleb rose with a grunt. "What's it to be then, sir?"

Morgan rolled his shoulders and stretched. Roland could hear cracking noises as he did it.

"General Arnold is planning to make a concerted charge at the British center. We're to provide covering fire and pick off any artillerymen. I'd like you two to take an eyeball at the spot and suggest where we can best set up."

Caleb grabbed his gear. "No sooner said than done, Colonel. I'll have the boy run back with the layout."

As Caleb and Roland moved through the woods, they could hear the sounds of battle starting in again. Gunfire sounded more often, and they could hear the shouts of men. They came to the edge of the dense woods. It was the same spot where the day's action had begun. A fair-sized clearing stretched around the area of Freeman's farm. Woods enclosed it on all sides. It was impossible to tell whose forces were in what location. Roland pulled out some writing paper and a piece of charcoal.

"I'm ready Caleb, how does it look to you?"

"All right then lad. The general's right, there's a gap between

Fraser and Hamilton. This wood surrounds the whole clearing except for that high spot. Could be a problem. Might let Fraser send help if he's not occupied. Can't tell for sure, but my guess is the British artillery units will be right at the edge of those trees to command this open ground."

"Where should we concentrate then Caleb?" asked Roland as he sketched.

"Well," said Caleb as he pulled off his hat and wiped some sweat from his forehead, "I'd say right about here, boy. Can you lead them back to this spot?"

"No problem."

Caleb sat down with his back against a tree. He sighed.

"Then off you go, lad. Be careful, eh?"

Roland raced off without a word.

Roland led the way back to the clearing, the main body of General Arnold's brigades following his lead. Once the infantry was in position, Morgan's riflemen, including Roland and Caleb, moved into the undergrowth at the edges of the clearing. Many of them climbed into the trees for better views. Roland lost track of Caleb in the confusion. He maneuvered as far east and north as he dared, to get close to the action. After climbing a maple tree, Roland could see across the clearing that British troops were moving. To his dismay, he could see they had moved some artillery into the spot Caleb had predicted. If they could get enough cannon into position, the British would fire grape shot into any American charge and cut the men to pieces.

Grape shot was one of Roland's great fears. You were unlikely to get smashed by a cannonball. Mortar and bombs could be bad. The enemy gunners would fire them to explode over top of your position and the shrapnel would rain down on you. But mortar and bombs were for a siege of a fort. It was hard to haul a mortar around in a field battle. There were howitzers, which were like mortars on wheels, but artillerymen said they were inaccurate, sometimes killing more of your own men than the enemy.

No, the real problem was grape shot and canister. Grape got

its name from the grape-sized lead balls formed around a wooden dowel. When the thing fired out of the cannon, it scattered everywhere. You could be way off to the side of the cannon and still catch a grape ball in your body. If you got hit by a full blast, it would tear you to pieces; Roland had seen a man shot with grape at Fort Ann. Cannister was almost the same. It was a container filled with lead balls and scrap metal and fired out of a cannon. Both had a kill zone up to 500 yards, which meant to get into rifle range you had to expose yourself to artillery fire. Roland didn't like that idea much.

Loading his rifle, Roland searched the edge of the clearing for a target. He didn't have to wait long. An artillery officer was moving his people into position. The officer had moved away from the tree that had been protecting him. A careless mistake. Roland drew up and waited for Morgan's signal.

From his left it came, the scattered fire that meant Morgan had turned his men loose. Roland fired too and saw the man go spinning to the ground. As he reloaded, he saw that the riflemen had concentrated their fire on artillerymen. They slumped dead or injured over the barrels, the wheels, or on the ground below. As usual, the sniper fire focused on officers. The cannon crews though were also beginning to panic. Roland fired again, this time not at a soldier but at the cannon itself; to give anyone considering approaching something to think about. Sparks flew as his bullet skimmed along the barrel. He saw the gun crew dive for the ground and allowed a satisfied smile to creep across his face.

Above the sounds of rifle fire, Roland heard the band pipe in. It was the infantry, the drums beating out a charge. From below and around him, Roland saw the Continental infantries rise and surge forward with bayonets fixed. They swarmed out of the woods onto the madness of the fighting ground of the clearing. From the woods to the north came the red coats of the British infantry to repulse the charge. Volley after volley of musket fire soon filled the air with dense smoke. Roland could see through the occasional openings in the smudge. The smoke drifted up and burned his eyes.

On the ground, the most intense fighting of the day had

begun. The American infantry moved forward and at first drove the British back. Their assault was fierce, and they overran the artillery positions. Some men turned the guns around to use on the retreating British, but the gunners had taken their charges and the guns were useless. With the success of the infantry, the riflemen moved along with them, trying to sweep off to the flanks.

Just when it looked like the American charge might work, reinforcements arrived from Fraser, off to the west. Burgoyne had taken an active role in the fighting and he reformed Hamilton's brigade into a counter charge. The American advance had stretched their line too thin and the British bayonet attack pushed them back in chaos. Each time the British charged the riflemen had to retreat full speed and maneuver their way behind the protection of the American infantry.

Roland could sense the flow of the battle. The riflemen could kill from a distance, but their rifles were slow to reload and couldn't be fitted with a bayonet. That meant if the British could get within range to close, the riflemen had to retreat. It was then the job of the light infantry to come forward and engage the British with their own bayonet charge and musket volleys.

The British had their riflemen too, but Roland could see right off they were no match for Morgan's men. Their rifles were little more accurate than a musket. The British strength was in their infantry charge using bayonets. They also responded to changes in the battle and regrouped faster than the Americans.

The battle swept back and forth across the clearing. Positions changed again and again as each side took, lost and retook the clearing and the woods. Each time the Americans advanced, the British reorganized and made a bayonet charge. There weren't enough American infantrymen engaged on the field to keep them off. But every time the British advanced they fell victim to the riflemen and by the time they had crossed the clearing, their number was down. That allowed the American infantry to counter charge. So, it went for hours under the September sun.

The smoke had filled the air for so long now that Roland thought he was breathing that alone. Each breath burned. It made his eyes water and the tears streaked his face as they cleaned off the smudges and dirt stuck to it. He had run out of water long ago.

There was a sudden tugging at his breeches. When he looked down, he saw his left pant leg had been shredded by a musket ball. *Hmm*, he thought, *looks like maybe the British have advanced again. I'd better fall back and try to find the rest of the riflemen.*

Keeping a careful grip on his rifle, Roland dropped to the ground.

He dropped right beside a British soldier. Both jumped back in surprise. The soldier was quicker to recover. He pointed his musket at Roland, standing less than five feet away, and fired. But no, a flash in the pan; the gun misfired, a brief flame and a puff of smoke. Roland stood with his mouth hanging open. This had happened to him before, but while hunting animals, never during a battle. His good luck had not yet registered when the British soldier attacked, slashing with his bayonet.

At the last second, Roland came to his senses. He leaped backward, coming up off the ground. The blade grazed across his chest, ripping through the buckskin shirt but only scratching his flesh. By the time his feet hit the ground again, Roland was running. This fighting was not for a rifleman and scout. This was the dirty work of infantry. He didn't slow down until he once again reached the security of Dearborn's tough infantrymen.

After a few minutes, the orders to advance came down once more. And once more Roland ran along the flanks. He tried to fight off his weariness and climbed a tree.

No one knew why, but the British had backed off. Arnold intended to take advantage of it. He thought perhaps they were low on ammunition. The Americans were too, but Arnold was determined to break the British line. Several charges had almost made it, but each time he had run out of men. Time after time he had asked Gates for reinforcements, but Gates was reluctant to risk too many men.

Roland reached a branch he liked. He took advantage of the break in the action to peek around. To his surprise, he could see Caleb in a tree not too far off. Overhead a crow flew by. As the bird moved past, a group of blackbirds rose from the trees. They chased after the crow and began ferocious dives at him. Despite his advantage in size, the blackbirds worked in concert and kept him from rising out of their range. Tired of the abuse, he veered off and flapped off for some safer spot.

Since things were still in a lull, Roland pulled out his spyglass. The smoke had cleared somewhat. He thought he might see what the British were doing. He scanned the edge of the woods. In a flash, he dropped the scope and turned toward Caleb, shouting at the top of his lungs.

"Grapeshot! Grapeshot! Take cover!"

It was too late. The roar of British cannon shook the area. The air filled with flying lead. It tore through the leaves, snapped saplings, smashed into trunks and bounced in fearsome ricochets from tree to tree.

Roland dropped his rifle to the ground and hugged himself to the tree's main trunk. He clamped his eyes so hard they hurt. He could hear the screams of men and the shudder of impact as several pieces of grapeshot blasted into his tree.

In seconds it was over, the field filled with smoke and the groans of wounded men. Roland checked Caleb's tree, but it was empty. He dropped to the ground and grabbed his rifle. Across the field came the sounds of a British charge. Roland felt his heart leap into his throat. He was sure the whole American army must have been destroyed.

But as he watched, he could see that many men were moving, though many were wounded. Wounded and able both had one thing on their minds- retreat. Roland too felt the panic. He looked left and right, not sure what he was looking for, but ready to run. A movement caught his eye, a wounded infantryman. Roland helped him to his feet.

"Thanks, I think I can still walk." said the soldier. He was more like a boy, no older than Roland. "Do you know which way to go?"

"Yes," said Roland. "But we've got to move fast, they'll be charging through here in a minute."

The soldier shook his head, then patted down the front of his body. He seemed to be inspecting himself.

"I can't seem to find where I got hit." he still sounded

confused.

Roland pointed. "Your head."

The man touched his head as if he thought it might fall off and pulled back a bloody hand. A small section of his scalp was ripped away. He scowled down at his hand.

"It doesn't hurt that bad."

"I think it will...later," said Roland. "Can you run? We must go."

They moved off, working their way toward the American line. The patriot army was in full retreat now, almost at a panic. The British were advancing, and the few men left fighting yielded the field and retreated into the woods.

Infantry and riflemen alike were walking as if dazed. *If the British get past the rear guard*, Roland thought, *this whole army might just bolt all the way to Albany.* But as these thoughts came, he heard a horse approaching and turned to see General Arnold on his stallion.

The General was in a frenzy. He raced his horse back and forth along the dejected Continental line, shouting encouragement, threats, and curses.

"We're not done yet, my brave boys!" he shouted.

Some of the men stopped.

"Johnny Burgoyne may think we'll turn and run at the first stiff fight, but now it's time to show him what a man's army is like." Hearing Arnold's voice was drawing the men together.

"Those red-coated King-lovers are sitting on their arses sipping tea right now. Who's ready to ruin their little tea party?!"

It was incredible, but Arnold had reassembled the retreating force. As more and more of the infantry came on the scene, they redressed into ranks. The men were from different groups, not the pure units of earlier, but they were responding to the officers. Roland saw riflemen too, running to join the action. Bayonets or no, they had been sparked by Arnold's charisma. Arnold jerked out his sword and his horse reared up. Roland could feel his skin prickle with pride and patriotism. With a wild cheer, the infantry was off in an all-out charge. Roland raced along with them.

The charge caught the British by complete surprise. They had thinned themselves in their last advance. Now the stalwart Americans broke them into three separate groups, flanking each. The British were driven back across the woods and into the clearing at Freeman's farm once again. Roland searched for Caleb as they moved along, but the speed of the advance was too great.

The infantry charged, fighting like wild men. They weren't in ranks any longer. There were no platoons or battalions, it was random groups of men fighting side by side. The riflemen swept off to the flanks and poured in their terrible fire. The British were bunched into clusters and the riflemen didn't even have to aim. They shot into the squirming mass at random.

The American infantry had closed the field. Their numbers now gave them the advantage. The British units were cut off from each other. If the attack could be maintained it seemed possible that the Americans would rout the British from the battlefield. Already bayonets were being fixed.

Roland's head was spinning as he loaded, shot and reloaded. He was dog tired. The constant stress of battle had taken its toll. A musket ball tore through his hat and he realized he was standing in the open. It no longer seemed to matter. All that mattered was to keep firing. He remained where he stuck to the spot and continued to reload. He fired a mindless blast into the British line and reloaded.

A new sound rising on the battleground brought him to his senses. At first, he couldn't believe his ears. He thought it was another part of the madness that had fallen on him. But the sound continued, got louder, and Roland stopped to listen.

The German force under von Riedesel was advancing, with the band playing at full blast as though it was a holiday. The surprised Americans paused in their attack. Arnold had again ridden off to ask for reinforcements. The unusual turn of events meant that no one seemed to know what to do. Before a response could be organized, the German riflemen, the "jaegers," arrived.

They were more effective than the British riflemen and the Americans had to turn their attention to them. As the American forces were divided, the British closed the breaks in their lines.

More German infantry arrived at the field and then artillery under the skilled command of Colonel Pausch. The Americans were still in disorder from their wild charge. Before they could reorganize, the field pieces were in position.

Again, Roland dove behind a tree as the terrifying grapeshot rained down from the German cannon. Blast after blast roared out and the Americans were brought to a halt. Roland sat trembling, his back against a tree. He peeked out once, to see an infantryman cut to pieces, his ruined body falling a few feet away. It was Captain Wilson from the N.Y. regiment. Yesterday they had been talking together of home. Wilson was only a couple of years older than Roland. He had spoken of his dream to run a general store, how he wanted to marry the blacksmith's daughter and have five children. Now all was gone. The hopes, the dreams, the future, all lay broken and bloodied on the battlefield.

At last, the cannon stopped. Roland's hearing seemed muffled as if his ears were filled with cotton. Something had hit him in the face and blood trickled from his cheek. The cut from the bayonet had leaked through, soaking his buckskin shirt. Rising to his feet made him feel a little unsteady. He saw many men moving across the field and through the woods. It was a full retreat, he could see that. But not in panic like before. The Americans were yielding the field in sullen dignity, in formation, with a rear guard holding off any British advance.

Roland moved with them. As they crossed the open area by Freeman's farm, he again looked for Caleb but saw no sign. It was getting dark. Soon the day's battle would be over. The British held the field. Tired but proud, Americans returned to their camp. Roland was exhausted.

CHAPTER TEN - AFTERMATH

Roland stopped, horrified by the scene. The American camp had descended into total chaos. Everything was complete disorganization. Men ran everywhere, no longer organized into regiments or companies. They had become a mass of confused, wounded, dirty, hungry men. Only a part of the total force had even been engaged during the day, but the movement of the reserves and the disorganization caused by the retreat had the whole army in a mess. Thinking Caleb might be wounded, Roland headed for the hospital.

The wounded lay in and around the hospital tent in various degrees of injury. As he made his way through, Roland was surprised to see that most had minor injuries. After the German grapeshot barrage, he was sure the American army was devastated. But, despite the many injuries, there seemed to be few corpses.

Roland recognized Dr. Thatcher hurrying among the confusion. As he rushed past, Roland grabbed his arm.

"Dr. Thatcher, have you seen Sergeant O'Connor?"

Thatcher never paused. He glared, then seemed to recognize Roland.

"I haven't seen your sergeant, son. Perhaps you should speak to Mrs. Owens."

Thatcher removed Roland's grasp and scurried off. Roland stood blinking for a few minutes. Then he noticed a large woman who seemed to be coordinating the tending to the wounded. He walked up to her.

"Excuse me, ma'am, are you Mrs. Owens?" Roland lifted his battered hat.

"Call me Mary, young man," she replied and reached out to turn his face. "The wounds on your face are minor. Nothing to worry about, there's nothing stuck in there. But we should get some salve for that slice on your chest and get it cleaned. The blood's all dried and I imagine your shirt's stuck to the wound. It'll hurt fierce when I pull off that buckskin."

"No, ma'am. I mean yes, ma'am, but that's not why I'm here. I'm looking for someone."

"Who might you be looking for?" she asked. She reminded him of his mother.

"I'm looking for my Sergeant. Sergeant O'Connor."

Mary nodded and in a loud, clear voice that rose above the din called out.

"I have a soldier here looking for a Sergeant O' Connor. Has anyone seen him?"

The words had just left her mouth when a girl came running toward them. She appeared to be about fifteen. Her fiery red hair swirled her head as she ran. Her face was flushed when she got there, and her eyes flashed like emeralds.

"What about Sergeant O'Connor?" she asked. She sounded out of breath.

"This young man is looking for him, Bridget," said Mary.

The green eyes bolted to Roland. "What do you mean, you're looking for him? Where is he?"

Roland was still groggy from the efforts of the day. He had to work to get the words out.

"Well, I, I... that's why I ...during the fight...I can't find him." he trailed off.

Faster than a rattlesnake, the girl reached out and grabbed Roland's arms.

"Look at me, Roland McCaffrey! You mean to say Da's lying out there somewhere? You left him there? And ran back home like a craven dog?!"

Roland's head was swimming. He couldn't follow the girl at all. *Da?*

Mary pulled the girl off him.

"Now Bridget, leave him be. Can't you see what he's been through?"

The girl jerked herself free of the large woman.

"But Mrs. Owens, you don't understand!" she said, tears filling her eyes. "That's my Da! Sergeant O'Connor!"

" But child, you never said..." replied Mrs. Owens and she put her arms around the now sobbing girl."

"He didn't want anyone to know." cried Bridget and she was sobbing again.

Roland stood puzzling at the two women for a moment. Then he turned and walked away in total confusion. *His daughter?* he thought. *No, it can't be. It must be another O' Connor.* But even as he thought it, he saw bits of the Irish soldier in this wild girl.

Darkness was setting in fast. Roland hurried to his tenting area. The acrid smell of smoke from cannon and musket had drifted from the battlefield into the camp. It mixed with the odors of sweat, blood, and fear. Roland was grateful to wash his face when he got to his gear. His head cleared a little and he drank the rest of the water. He rummaged through his haversack and found a chunk of bread and some salt pork. Even that poor fare went down with ease. He noticed a pot with the morning's leftover coffee. Roland drained the bitter remains.

When he had soothed his hunger and thirst, he noticed Caleb's gear still sitting untouched. *Maybe he's reporting to Colburn,* he thought, *I wonder if that's where I should be.*

With a groan, Roland shouldered his rifle and pouch and moved through the camp to Colonel Colburn's tent. Officers and men were running and shouting everywhere. Several times men stopped to ask him if he had seen any of their regiments. Roland thought to himself *if the British were to attack at this moment, the whole American Northern Department would surrender at once.* No one knew where their officers were, where the ammunition was, or even where their friends were. Roland doubted if he had enough powder for two rounds. Any attack would have to be repulsed with bare hands.

Colburn's tent presented another jumble of confusion. Scouts were milling around, most in the same shape as Roland. Unlike much of the American force, most of the scouts had been involved in the day's battles. Roland recognized Jimmy Williams and went up to him. Williams was sitting against one of the tent poles, holding a rag to his shoulder.

"Are you all right Jimmy?" asked Roland.

"Dammed bloody grapeshot ripped my shoulder," he growled.

"Can I help at all?"

"No, it'll be fine Rollie, I'm just angry," said Jimmy, and then whispered, "and scared."

Roland squatted next to him.

"Why?" he asked, also whispering.

Williams gestured with his head. "Nobody knows where they're supposed to be. We're all out of cartridges, half the officers are trying to herd up their men, the other half are huddled with the General at the fort. My grandma and two banty roosters could take this bunch right now."

"I know, I was thinking the same thing. What about us? I can't find Caleb. Do you think he might be in with the Colonel?"

Williams shook his head at Roland, his face tight and pale.

"Colburn's missing, Rollie."

Roland's throat tightened. He knew men would die in battle. He had even seen some men he knew fall. But Colonel Colburn had seemed invincible. The man would scout at night in Indian territory alone. It was unthinkable that anything could have happened to him.

"Maybe they're together." he sighed.

"I hope not," said Williams, "'cause if they are, there's only one place they'd be now."

Roland rose and patted his friend's head.

"Take care of yourself, Jimmy. I've got to get going."

"You too, Rollie."

Roland wasn't sure what to do next. It wasn't easy to think under these conditions. He would check in at Colonel Morgan's tent. Perhaps he'd even find Caleb there.

Morgan's camp was at least more organized. His men were regrouping at the site. They were fixing some food, and some were already sleeping among the noise and confusion. But Morgan himself was at Fort Neilson with Arnold and Gates, tallying the days' action.

Worry and fatigue were catching up to Roland. He could feel the tears welling up in his eyes. He thought of his father and mother. If his father were here now, he'd know what to do, who to see. His head swam, and he sat down right in the middle of the camp. Roland stared off into space and let his mind crawl to a halt. *Who is that girl? Why didn't Caleb tell me? She's right, I am a coward to leave him out there. How did she know who I was?*

After a few minutes, his eyes could focus again, and he realized he was seeing the small encampment of Oneida Indians at the edge of the main grounds. The Oneidas were one of the Iroquois tribes who had joined up with the Americans rather than the British. There was a small group with them now who acted as scouts. Roland knew several of the braves. He rose, brushed off his clothes, and walked to their camp.

Talking Owl saw him coming and several of the other men rose to greet him.

"Little Longrifle, welcome. Come, you tired, sit," said Talking Owl.

Roland could speak little Oneida but Talking Owl had learned English and spoke it well.

"No, I can't stay Talking Owl. I am troubled."

"I am sorry to hear that, Little Longrifle. Can we ease your trouble?"

"I hope so, Talking Owl, I have come to you to ask for help. My friend is missing."

"Ah, the Irish. Big Longrifle," said Talking Owl.

Roland nodded, and despite himself, a tear dribbled from one eye. Talking Owl turned and spoke to a couple of the braves. He put his hand on Roland's shoulder.

"Then let us talk no more. Come, let us find him."

Total darkness had set in when Roland and the three Oneidas arrived back at the fighting ground. Along the way, they had come upon John Neilson, who had insisted on helping. He told Roland that there "weren't no spot" in the area he couldn't find a missing man. Roland accepted the offer with gratitude.

This scene appeared even more horrific than the camp. Here, the dead and dying lay all around. As the small group moved through the darkness, they could hear an occasional moan or cough. The dead seemed to be underfoot everywhere. As they searched, Roland realized that the day's battle had gone for the Americans. Dead British soldiers littered the woods and fields. Dozens more lay wounded or dying. But their mission was not killing tonight, and Roland even offered a drink of water to a British soldier he stumbled over in the dark. The man nodded in thanks and crumpled over, dead.

One of the braves tapped Roland's shoulder and pointed off into the night. As Roland tried to see, he made out Neilson waving them over. Like silent ghosts, they moved among the bodies. Neilson pointed, and Roland followed his finger.

There! Caleb sat leaning back against a tree, sipping at his flask. Asleep beside him was Colonel Colburn. Roland moved nearer, then whistled. He didn't want Caleb to react and shoot him. Caleb flinched, raised his rifle, and looked up. Roland moved his hand and Caleb saw him. He lowered the weapon and let his head fall back against the tree trunk. The search party hurried over.

"Praise the Lord, child, whatever are you doing out on this hellish night?"

Roland had to smile. "We're looking for you, Sergeant. I thought I'd lost you, Caleb. You and the Colonel both. Wake him up and let's be out of here. Are you all right?"

Caleb patted Roland's face. "Aye, I'm mere scraped lad. Oh, a small hole in me arm. But the Colonel here, well, he's sleeping the Long sleep, I'm afraid."

Roland peered at Colburn, then back at Caleb. "He's dead?"

Caleb struggled to his feet.

"When the cannon fire blasted us, it took me out of the tree. Only a piece in the arm, but I was stunned when I hit the ground. When I come to, there's the Colonel with me. He got me against this tree, helped me with a bandage. After a few minutes, I start to come clear and I see he's shot through, bleedin' like a stuck pig. Wasn't no point in trying to get home, the woods crawling with British. So, we waited it out. But the wait took too long. He passed on. It didn't feel right to leave him till it was over. By then it's all dark, and I could hear the lobsterbacks poking all about."

Caleb nodded at Colburn, propped against the tree. He looked peaceful.

"Good man, the Colonel. War's a hard thing, son."

Roland was still looking at Colburn trying not to believe he was gone. Talking Owl appeared out of nowhere. He spoke to Caleb.

"Redcoats and Mohawks. Coming here, we must go. Big Longrifle, I am glad you live."

"I am glad too, Talking Owl, I'm glad too."

Caleb reached down and pulled Colburn's pack off. He reached inside the Colonel's coat and took out his diary. He knew the Colonel was a literate man. His family would want words to remember him by. Colburn had written the last entry as he lay with Caleb, dying in the autumn night.

Caleb nodded to Talking Owl and the men moved off through the death and darkness, back to the American encampment.

CHAPTER ELEVEN - THE DAY AFTER

Roland was again moving across the gloomy battlefield among the dead. It seemed even darker than before, and he kept tripping over bodies. He kept searching for Colburn. He was convinced the Colonel lay there somewhere, still alive. Roland needed to find him before it was too late. In the darkness, he could hear someone calling his name.

"Roland... Roland." the voice called.

Roland moved toward the voice. With a start, he realized he'd forgotten his rifle. The voice spoke again, right next to him and he jumped. Then he froze in fear as he saw that the voice was coming from a dead man at his feet. Terror clutched at him as the dead man groaned and moved into a sitting position. The dead eyes rolled up at Roland.

"Why Roland, why?" asked the corpse.

Roland understood and replied, "I'm sorry, it's war." His voice shook.

The corpse shook its head, "Is that an excuse to kill a man? I had a family too, you know. How long will they wait for me, not even knowing I'm dead in this godforsaken place? Why did you have to kill me, Roland?"

A deep sadness fell over him as he imagined the dead man's wife and children, sitting around a table, waiting for word of their lost husband and father.

"It's not my fault. Why did you have to come here? Why couldn't you leave us to our own? Why didn't you stay with your family?" Roland was shouting now.

"What of me, Roland?" asked another voice. Another dead man had walked up to them. This one Roland even recognized. It was a young soldier he'd killed at the Freeman's farm clearing. "It was the army or prison for me. I didn't want to be here, but what choice did I have?"

Roland felt himself becoming angry. He pulled his pistol out of the waist of his pants.

"It's not my fault!" he shouted, "I'm defending my country and standing up for what I believe in!"

"All you believe in is killing!" yelled yet another corpse, this one the young Indian brave Roland had killed at Crown Point. It seemed a lifetime ago.

"Murderer!" came the cry from another walking dead man. Roland whirled and pointed the pistol. It was the tall Grenadier.

"Hold your ground," he said to the last corpse.

"Or you'll kill me?" asked the corpse, "Again?" He moved toward Roland.

"So be it," said Roland. The roar of his pistol filled the air.

Roland woke with a start. He noticed he was grasping his pistol and tossed it aside. Though the night had been cool, he dripped with sweat. Dawn was breaking, and the camp sounded like it was still in turmoil. He breathed easier as he realized he had been dreaming. Across the smoldering fire, Caleb sat drinking from his flask, watching Roland. The smoke swirled around his grim face.

"Bad dreams, eh child?" he asked.

"Very bad," replied Roland.

"Happens to all men after a battle, son. Don't let it worry you. If the dead didn't talk to you, then I'd be worried."

"But how did you...?"

"What else?" Caleb shrugged. "Come, have some breakfast. I'm afeared the devil will have his due today. Best to see it through on a full belly."

"Caleb, yesterday, at the hospital, I met a girl."

"Aye, lad. I heard about that; I did."

"She said you were her Da."

"Ah. Well, she would now, wouldn't she? Seein' as how I am."

"But you never said you had a family."

Caleb shrugged and got to his feet.

"Well lad, never seemed much point in bringin' it up. Not a

family anyway, just the girl."

"But you mean she's been here, with the army all this time, and you never said anything?" Roland was outraged.

Color flashed in the big man's face.

"Now listen, child. Not every man's got a nice, happy family like you. You don't even know how lucky you are. Some men don't have a story they care to blab about with a bunch of half-wit soldiers."

Roland stared down at his feet.

"You're right Sergeant. It's none of my business. I didn't mean to pry, I'm sorry."

Caleb turned and kicked at the fire.

"Bloody hell, boy! I didn't mean that!" He walked over to Roland and knelt on one knee. He rested one of his great hands on the boy's shoulder. He spoke with an unexpected gentleness.

"Her mother's not around, child. A girl without her mother, well, she's got no one to watch out for her. I'm no good, always gone out creeping around. Just thought it'd better if no one knew. I'm the one who's sorry. 'specially after you come lookin' for me last night. That was foolish, child, foolish. But I'm much obliged."

Roland shook his head.

"I won't tell anyone, Caleb, I promise."

Caleb stood. "Ah, won't matter now anyhow. That gossipy Mrs. Owens knows now and that means all them hens'll be cooing around her, 'Oooo, poor girl, no mother, that ugly drunken sergeant for a father,' Ah, well."

Roland moved to stand, and a pain reminded him of the wound on his chest. When he looked down, it surprised him to see it was bandaged. Caleb grunted.

"Aye, she came by early this morning. Mean as a snake, she was. Scolded me for not telling you about her. Felt like the little fool she is for makin' a scene at the hospital, more so when she heard you went back out looking for me. Here, she did this too. In the way of apology, I suppose. Got her mother's temper all right."

Caleb tossed Roland his hunting shirt. The rip from the bayonet had been patched.

"She?" asked Roland. "You mean Bridget? Your daughter?"

"None other. Come, boy, let's be getting ready. There'll be confusion in the ranks today. We'd be wise to be ready for anything."

Roland pulled on his shirt and gathered his gear. The flowing red hair and flashing emerald eyes danced through his mind. She had come before he awoke and bandaged his wounds and repaired his shirt. A strange feeling came through him and he realized he wanted to see the fierce Bridget O'Connor again. He saw Caleb, shouldering his pack. *His daughter?* Roland shook his head and plopped on his sad hat.

At Fort Neilson, Gates and his field commanders had been up most of the night. Troop movements, ammunition movements, and reassignments had kept on till dawn. The Americans were in no shape to repel an attack. The western heights had still not been adequately fortified. A full-scale British assault could take it. The left wing had taken a hard hit, though deaths were light. Sixty-five men were killed on the day's action, a low number considering over five hours of constant engagement. But there were over 200 wounded, and regiments had to be re-positioned. That hadn't gone smooth and a strike, even at the American center, might be a disaster.

But nothing had been lost either. Gates still held the better ground, had dependable supply lines, and a motivated army. Nighttime scouting parties had reported that enemy losses were high. The dead lay everywhere in large numbers. The American withdrawal had seemed a defeat yesterday, but now, considering the numbers, it seemed a great tactical success.

At his headquarters, General Burgoyne was ready to go. He still said that a strong assault on the American left could succeed. Those heights were the key to this position. If not for that damned Arnold, it could have already been his.

But Burgoyne was also troubled by doubts. He'd not been prepared for the American riflemen. They had almost wiped out his artillery units. When General Phillips had ridden to the front yesterday, he found only one surviving officer still at his gun. The American infantry, too, had shown their courage, often going volley for volley at close range with some of Burgoyne's best troops. This would not be an easy victory of the sort he'd experienced at Ticonderoga.

British losses had been much worse than Burgoyne could have envisioned. There were over 600 dead, missing or wounded. Among the dead, a high number had been officers. The accuracy of the American riflemen had been devastating. Burgoyne was reluctant to give the foreigner credit, but if not for vonRiedesel, the day could have been lost.

His generals were of mixed opinion, some for another attack, others in favor of at least a day of rest.

In the end, both Burgoyne and Gates waited. Each had their armies break camp and prepare for action, expecting the other to attack. The next day, the 21st of September, each General received a messenger that would influence their next steps.

From General Howe in New York came a message to Burgoyne that Sir Henry Clinton would make a move into the Hudson highlands north of his position. It was the British Generals' hope that such an attack would force Gates to send men south to help protect the lower Hudson valley. Burgoyne, realizing he was now outnumbered, chose to wait for Clinton's diversion. When Gates sent men south, weakening his force, Burgoyne would attack.

Gates, however, received information that convinced him he could outwait Burgoyne. It was news from General Benjamin Lincoln. Lincoln had been sent out with a force to harass Burgoyne's supply line from Ticonderoga. Along the way, he had taken Fort George in a surprise attack and moved undetected up to Fort Ticonderoga. His forces had taken both of the fortified hilltops. As a joke, Lincoln had called on the fort to surrender. When his call was rejected, Lincoln had responded by destroying 200 bateaux, 17 armed ships and vast quantities of provisions. With his bold foray, Lincoln had cut off Burgoyne's supplies.

Upon hearing of Lincoln's raid, a loud cheering went up from the American forces. With the closeness of the lines, the cheers were heard by Burgoyne at his headquarters. He wondered what ill wind had come blowing his way next.

CHAPTER TWELVE - ENTRENCHMENT

The waiting game went on far longer than either general expected. By day the American scouts were sent out on regular rounds to check on the British activity. They were hard at work. Three large redoubts had been built. The largest, the Great Redoubt, was now Burgoyne's headquarters. Huge rows of earthen barriers, shoulder high, were reinforced with wood and stone. It was constructed to be a fort. Within the redoubt was the main British camp.

The second redoubt, called the Balcarres Redoubt, was named after the major in charge, the dashing Earl of Balcarres. It sat in the area around Freeman's farm. This redoubt too was a massive earthen structure. Its design would provide both cover and protected positions from which to use the artillery. All around the redoubt, the British had cut down trees to make more open areas. This made the redoubt difficult to assault and the open ground favored the British fighting style.

The third redoubt was called the Breymann Redoubt, after the German officer in command, the brutal Heinrich von Breymann. He provoked fear and hated both his men and the enemy. His reputation as a cruel bully was known even to the Americans. This redoubt had been constructed from logs rather than dirt. Between the Breymann and Balcarres redoubts sat a cabin. This had been fortified and manned by a force of Canadians.

The Americans too were hard at work. They had fortified the western heights with earthen walls and cannon. It now presented a formidable target to take. Men had continued to pour into camp. Gates's forces now numbered near 11,000 men, double the troops Burgoyne had available. Earth walls were being constructed, trenches dug, and materials moved from spot to spot. Roland's days were occupied scouting and digging trenches.

He was laboring under the early fall sun when he heard a familiar voice.

"So young Mr. McCaffrey, I see you're a hard worker as well as a good shot."

Roland smiled and looked up. "Miss O'Connor, a pleasure to see you again."

"I doubt that very much, sir. And my name's Bridget, as you well know."

She plopped on the ground above the trench.

"Here, I've brought you some water. And my apologies too, I might as well say. I've an evil temper. That's no excuse, mind you. I said some horrible things to you and for that, I'm much ashamed. My mother was a witch you know, has Da told you her? It's from her my temper comes. Can you not talk, boy?"

Roland took a drink of the water.

"Not like you," he replied.

Bridget beamed a smile and giggled. Roland noticed a funny twinge go through his chest. He climbed out of the trench and sat down next to Bridget.

The breeze was blowing her hair and she had to hold it back with one hand to see him. As Roland looked at her, he noticed she was a burst of colors. The red hair, the green eyes, the freckles brought out by the summer sun, the even, white teeth, the red lips. *How beautiful she is,* he thought, surprising himself.

"Have you been with the army since Ticonderoga? he asked.

"Oh no. I came up from Albany with some of the women when you come south. That's where I stay mostly, Albany. I live with a family who's friends of Da. Not planning to stay there for long, though. Think I'll be headin' to the west, to the wilderness. I want to see more of this country. A place big as this, doesn't seem like a person should hide in the one place, does it? Are you plannin' to be a farmer, then? Or a soldier?"

She went too fast for Roland. He was nervous enough talking with any girl, but this here was Caleb's daughter. Besides, she talked such a streak he couldn't make up a reply to one thing before she jumped off to the next.

"Well, no. I'm no good at farming. And I'm not so good at

soldiering, either."

"No? That's not what Da, says. He says you're the best rifleman in the army. And the quietest scout. And the best educated rifleman too. I can read and write, too. Do you think it's all right for a woman to learn to shoot? I can shoot, too, you know, Da taught me, though he don't think it's proper."

"I guess I hadn't thought about it that much."

"Well it wouldn't hurt you to think about something besides rifles, you know. Got to go; can't stay here with you all day, though I wouldn't mind. Got to get back to the hospital."

She leaned over and kissed him lightly on the cheek.

"Thanks for gettin' me Da."

She jumped up and floated away like the wind. Roland wasn't sure she had even been there. He'd never met anyone like her before. He went back to the trench but all afternoon his mind kept turning to the little red-haired girl with so much to say.

Each night the riflemen were sent out to harass the enemy. Roland often went with them, being both a skilled scout and deadly sniper. It was easy to get within range of the British positions. Not a night went by when they didn't kill a few guards who got careless. The riflemen also made it a point to appear on the scene at mealtimes, making cooking a dangerous affair, even at the well-manned Balcarres Redoubt. Any attempt by the British to send out troops to attack the snipers was unsuccessful. The riflemen melted into the woods where the British feared to pursue.

One evening a group of Morgan's men asked Roland to come with them to the Breymann Redoubt. Earlier in the day, they had spotted a group of Germans working further out from the Redoubt than usual. Morgan wanted to know what they had been up to. When the scouting party arrived, Wallace Travers told the others to stay out of sight. He handed his rifle to Roland.

"Hang on to this for me, I want to move quick tonight," said Travers.

Travers pulled a huge knife out and moved off into the darkness. The rest of the group waited in nervous anticipation.

"What's he doing, anyway?" Roland asked one of the riflemen. The man scowled and nodded into the night.

"With Wallace, you never know," he said. "He speaks German, maybe he's hangin' around the edge of their camp to tryin' to hear what they're planning."

A few minutes later, Travers reappeared. He was grinning from ear to ear and wearing one of the tall, pointed German helmets. Even in the faint moonlight, Roland could see blood spattered on Travers' face. He thought of what Caleb had told him of the man.

"Nice hat, Wallace. Looks good on you, maybe you should join the Hessians. Where'd you get it anyhow?" asked one the other men.

Travers again pulled out his knife and wiped it off on a piece of blue cloth.

"From some blood money mercenary who got more than he bargained for. Let's go, they ain't up to anything."

From that night on, Roland viewed Travers in a different light.

Roland's nightmares continued as new faces were added to his evening talks with the dead. By their frequency alone, Roland became used to them. After a while, he talked to the ghosts about their families and discuss his own with them. The dreams became as much relief as terror. He used them to explain to the dead why he had to kill them and to apologize for it. He realized it was not too different from the Iroquois when they killed a deer and then explained to the deer's spirit why the death had been necessary. Roland talked to Caleb, explaining the change in his dreams.

"It's strange, Caleb. At first, my greatest fear was that I wouldn't be able to fight again, that I would be useless as a soldier. Now, do you know what I fear most?"

Caleb peered down at Roland over his pipe.

"You're afraid that you like the killing."

Roland was taken by surprise. He hadn't mentioned this to anyone.

"That's right, but how did you know?"

"Because you're good at it."

Roland nodded and kicked at the ground. It was true. Not yet eighteen and he couldn't keep track of the number of men he'd killed. He wasn't bloodthirsty, but he always seemed to be in the middle of the action, and his aim was true.

"Is it true then Caleb? Am I a born killer? A murderer?"

"No child, you're no murderer. You're a soldier. But I must admit, I'm damned glad you're on my side. It don't pay to wear a red coat and cross your path and that's a fact."

Roland started to reply when Bridget came rushing up to them.

"Da! Ye won't believe what just happened!"

Caleb rose and put his arm around his daughter. "Settle down girl. Here, sit and tell what's got you so riled."

She took a couple of deep breaths.

"Well, you know how sometimes I help with the serving in the Fort? Well, tonight I was helping, and they were all there, all the officers. General Gates was having his pie when General Arnold comes stomping in. Well, he's all worked up about something and says how he, Gates, didn't say anything in his letter to the Congress about how his wing was the main part of the army that won the day in the big battle. And Gates, he acts like he doesn't know what Arnold is talking about and that makes him, Arnold that is, even madder. Then they get to arguing about who's to command the left wing and Gates says to Arnold that he don't even know for sure if Arnold _is_ a General. Arnold's face is turning so red I think he'll blow like a hot cannon. Can you imagine anyone sayin' such things to the General? Well, then General Gates tells Arnold that he's putting General Lincoln in charge of the left wing and Morgan's men will be under himself's own command. He says he has nothing for General Arnold to do. And then, Arnold says he'll write to the Congress to ask to be sent to General Washington where he can fight instead of sitting around. Then Gates says to him well do what he has to do. And then Arnold storms out. And then I come runnin' down here to tell you. But Da, I got to go back up, because I got to clean up after the officers. Are ye goin' out tonight, Roland?"

Roland's mouth was hanging open and he nodded. His brain

was too slow again.

"Then you be careful, I'd not want anything to happen to you. And keep track of Da, will you?" She touched the side of his head for a second, kissed her father and was gone.

"Caleb?" asked Roland.

Caleb shook his head. "Her mother was like that too, lad."

"No, I mean... well, I mean that too, but all that with General Arnold?"

"Ah. Well, you know, child, it's like I've told you. No sane man can predict what an officer might do. Those two are like fire and ice, bound to come to a bad end. Still, I'd not like to see Arnold leave us. Not with Johnny still lurkin' about."

Roland thought this news over. This was unexpected. Everything had gotten complicated; vanBrocklin, Colburn, Bridget, Arnold, the ghosts. He even wished the clear-cut madness of battle would come again. Not this nighttime sniper action, but something major. Something that would bring Gentleman Johnny out into the open and settle this thing once and for all.

On the night of October 6, John Burgoyne was doing some serious thinking himself. His army was starving, the Americans had cut him off from his supply line. Every day more of the rebels arrived at the area. Each day more of his men deserted or died of disease or hunger. At night the American snipers picked off more guards. His men were at a point of refusing guard duty. Arrest sounded better than death. Clinton's raids in the Hudson highlands had succeeded, but Gates had not been drawn off. The only good news was the word that Arnold had been relieved of command. He was their most skilled tactician. "Granny" Gates would be cautious, indecisive. That would allow Burgoyne to dictate when the next action would take place.

The time was now or never. Burgoyne refused to crawl back to Canada with his tail between his legs. He could still make Albany, crush the rebellion and still be the hero. Throwing back his shoulders, Burgoyne sent an aide to summon his Generals.

CHAPTER THIRTEEN - BEMIS HEIGHTS

Roland moved like a stalking panther through the woods. It was October 7, 1777, and the British were on the move in force. At the sound of a signal gun, it seemed all the men in the Balcarres and Breymann redoubts marched out. They were bringing cannon, too, at least ten pieces. Roland ran up to the next man in the scouting relay and passed on the information. Then he moved back to keep an eye on the enemy movements.

It was a major advance, the one they had been waiting for. It had to be over 1500 men, including Grenadiers, light infantry, and Hessians This had to be the real thing. Roland and the other scouts fell back as when they saw which direction their march was taking. Roland found Caleb.

"They're coming, Caleb. Marching from both redoubts in force. Grenadiers and cannon too." said Roland. "Where are they headed, son?" asked the Sergeant.

"I can't be sure, but it looks like they're headed for the heights again."

"Here?" said Caleb in amazement. "Can't they see we've fortified?"

"I don't know," replied Roland. "It don't look like they've got any scouts left, there's nobody out front. Maybe they don't know."

The British force moved out in formation. They left the two redoubts, passed the Canadian cabins and spread into two separate clearings. There were some abandoned huts along the edge. Next to them, was a large wheat field. There, the British troops came to a halt. A group of soldiers moved into the wheat and cut some down. It was well known the British had a food shortage and their horses, too, were starving. As the men worked, a group of officers climbed to the tops of the cabins and pulled out their spyglasses.

Roland, too, was watching the officers. To his surprise, he could see Generals Fraser, Phillips, and vonRiedesel. *If only they were in range*, he thought. The sunlight flashed off their glass as they turned up to the western heights. *They can see our guns up there now. I wonder what they'll do? Turn back?* Roland thought to himself.

It seemed that the British officers were wondering the same thing, for the entire force came to a rest along the clearings. After a few minutes, their line widened both east and west until it formed a long, thin line over a thousand yards long.

"They're extending their line," called Roland down from his tree to the men below. "It's long, too long, they can never hold it. We've got to let General Gates know before they move more men up!"

No sooner were the words out of Roland's mouth than a messenger was racing to Fort Neilson to inform Gates of the British movements.

At Fort Neilson, Gates remained hesitant to commit his hand. Although he now had a great advantage in numbers, he still knew the British troops were better battle trained than his mix of regular army and militia.

"General? What are your orders?" asked General Lincoln. Lincoln was now in command of the left wing, having relieved Arnold under Gates' orders.

Gates remained silent. He studied the map, read through the scouts' reports and leaned back in his chair.

"I am still considering options, General Lincoln. Enoch," Gates turned to General Poor, "what say you? Do we risk attack?"

Poor tried to assess the men in the room. Lincoln was unsure of himself in front of Gates. Even after his success at Ticonderoga, he hesitated to voice an opinion. General Learned was a tough man, he was ready to go, but he was playing the game, his face frozen and impossible to read. Morgan was chomping at the bit. He was like Arnold, always ready for action. Poor

himself, was ready for a fight, but he didn't much want to make such an important decision. His gaze wandered back to General Benjamin Lincoln.

"Well General," said Poor, turning to Gates, "the numbers and the lay of the field are to our advantage. But the action would fall most heavily on the left wing. If General Lincoln is ready to go, then..."

Everyone turned to Lincoln. He shot a quick glance at Morgan, who gave a small nod.

"We are more than ready, General Gates. Our scouts are in position and have already marked the ground. If I may deploy Colonel Morgan and Major Dearborn, we can have men in position before the hour."

Gates sighed at his map. He put his face in his hands and took a deep breath. He could feel the weight of history bearing down on him. Something inside him whispered that his decision would resonate through time, for good or evil. He stood, straightened his coat, and turned to his officers.

"Colonel Morgan, it is time to begin the game."

Morgan raced from the room to gather his riflemen. Outside, he stopped to write a short note to General Arnold. He owed it to his old friend to let him know what was going on.

Back inside, Gates turned to Poor and Learned.

"Gentlemen, let us make the day."

As the battle began, Gates put over nine-thousand men into action just after noon.

CHAPTER FOURTEEN - THE BATTLE OF BEMIS HEIGHTS PART 1

Roland waited for the signal. He had moved out with Morgan's riflemen and Dearborn's infantry to high ground above the British position. From here he could see the layout of the British line. They had a good position. Their cannon commanded a large open area suitable for European style combat, with ranks of infantry and bayonet charges. But the openings were surrounded by wooded areas. These would offer protection for the Americans

Caleb appeared out of the underbrush like a great red-haired bear. Roland could smell the whiskey as Caleb kneeled beside him.

"All right, Rollie boy. It's like this. Morgan wants to move around the Brits right wing. If we can, he wants to get in behind 'em. We'll drive them through the thickets and right into Learned's boys."

"It's Fraser again, Caleb. The grenadiers."

"Ah, well child. There's little glory in besting your lessers. Anyway, I got a feelin' the Old Waggoner finds the heart of the battle wherever he's assigned."

Caleb rose to his feet. He pulled off his cap and wiped his brow with a shirt sleeve. Although many of the leaves were already in color, it was a warm autumn morning. The big Irishman spat and took another sip from his whiskey flask.

"Is everything all right, Caleb?" asked Roland.

Caleb nodded at the flask and nodded down at Roland.

"Aye, lad. I've been at it early today, eh?" He tucked the flask away inside his shirt. "I've an ill feelin' on the day, is what it is. Can't seem to shake it. Still..." He plopped his cap back on. "It's out of our hands anyway, ain't it, Rollie?"

"Where do I go, Caleb?" asked Roland. The bad feeling was catching, and he found his palms were sweating.

"This runnin' around's easier for you than me. Why don't you take Travers' group and see how far around their backsides you can get? Wait for the shootin' to start. That'll be Morgan's signal."

"He scares me sometimes, Caleb."

Caleb raised an eyebrow. "Meanin' Travers, I take it."

"Yes. He's a deadeye-shot and he moves like a cat. But there's something about him. Still, he's always done right by me."

"Well child, war brings out hidden feelings in us all. For some, all the killin' makes life look cheap. For others, it makes it all the more precious." He slapped Roland on the shoulder. "You'd best be on your way."

The cover was ideal for the Americans. The trees hid the riflemen and allowed Dearborn's light infantry to move unseen into close range. It was early afternoon when the attack began. Morgan unleashed his riflemen. The British fell under the devastating assault. They were caught off guard. No sooner had the first wave of rifle bullets hit than Dearborn's men fired off a volley of musket balls at close range and swept down from the rise.

From off to his right, Roland could hear the shouts as Poor's brigade attacked the British left. Moments later, Learned's brigade moved into action in the center. The Americans engaged the British force with a three to one advantage in numbers.

Poor's men hit at Major Aclund's Grenadiers, one of the toughest fighting groups in the British army. The Americans were charging uphill and the enemy fire went high. First, the musket volley and then the grapeshot went sailing over the heads of the cheering rebels. The Grenadiers reloaded their muskets, but the Americans had held their fire until they were at the crest of the slope. With several swift volleys, Poor's men staggered the mighty British ranks.

This was a proud group of Grenadiers and they regrouped and returned fire. Their efforts only seemed to work the attacking Americans into a frenzy. They swept over the hill, routing the British into a wild retreat. Several men turned a captured British cannon around and the retreating redcoats were riddled by their own grapeshot as they ran.

Meanwhile, a group of riflemen under Travers' command had slipped all the way around the British line. Under Roland's direction, they stalked their prey like a pack of wolves. They encircled Fraser's rear guard. Travers appeared next to Roland.

"The famous British Grenadiers, eh McCaffrey? Well, let's see how fast they can run in them funny hats." He raised his rifle and fired.

The bullets seemed to come from everywhere. The Englishmen were cut down like harvest corn. A couple tried to return fire but had no targets. They were soon gunned down and, with that, the rest took off like jackrabbits through the woods. The riflemen shouted and fired a few shots through the trees just to keep them moving.

After the initial attack, Morgan regrouped the riflemen. They maneuvered through the woods onto the flank of the troops commanded by the young Earl of Balcarres. Taking cover along a wooden rail fence, they poured bullets into the unprotected British infantry. Caught by surprise, Balcarres' men huddled together, uncertain where the attack was coming from or where a retreat path lay. Roland was no longer taking careful aim at specific targets, but firing into the mass of men retreating before him. Balcarres' men were trying to return fire, but the riflemen kept out of musket range and behind the fence and trees.

Reloading, Roland could see a change in the British movements. From within the mass, someone was organizing men into ranks. Roland laid his rifle on the fence and scanned the enemy, trying to identify the officer in charge. He found him. He was moving men around, encouraging them and arranging a charge at the American position. It had to be the Earl.

Roland fired. Balcarres flinched and spun around but Roland could see he'd only torn a hole in the Earl's coat. Before reloading he took another look at the brave man, valiantly trying to rally his men.

With a roar, Dearborn's men rose to their feet. Under the cover of the riflemen's attack, they had advanced right on top of Balcarres' position. Almost as one, they blasted a series of volleys and it was the end for Balcarres' men. They scattered from the field in a full retreat to the redoubt. Dozens of dead and wounded lay among the bloodied autumn leaves.

A shout went up from the Americans and they began a disorganized pursuit. Ranks had been broken and Roland ran along with a group of infantrymen. Flush with their success at routing the famed Earl of Balcarres, the men had lost all discipline and turned into a mob. They fired at random into the retreating British. After a few minutes, the pace slowed, and things calmed down. Roland could hear Morgan's voice booming above the sounds of battle.

"Riflemen! Riflemen!" he bellowed.

The infantry drummers were beating out instructions to reform. With their troops at last back under control, Morgan and Dearborn advanced in formation. Soon they came on Learned's men. This was now the tipping point of the battle. Here, the tough German troops under Baron vonRiedesel were holding their ground.

Roland, taking advantage of the break in the action, pulled out his spyglass. Looking at the German position, he could see the little German commander himself. von Riedesel moved among his men, moving a man here, a man there, keeping the ranks solid and men under control.

"What's it look like, child?" Caleb's rough voice asked. Roland jumped. He hadn't noticed Caleb's arrival. Again, he marveled at the speed and stealth of his giant sergeant.

"That fat little baron shows no fear, Sergeant. Those Hessians are tough men. The British on both sides have retreated but they fight on. I can see jaegers in there too. We'll be in their range if we move much closer."

"Aye, but that's sure and what we'll be doin' lad and soon I'm thinking."

Caleb was right. Orders were coming down the line as he spoke. Caleb listened to the instructions and called Roland and the other scouts to gather round.

"All right lads, it's simple. The infantry will charge. We're to spread out, get the riflemen on the flanks, and fire at will. Follow their lead, go after the jaegers and the artillerymen. The closer we can get our boys the better it'll go. Now move, Dearborn's boys are getting ready."

Roland was a fast runner. He raced out to the extreme edge of the American line. When he stopped, he was almost behind the Germans. As usual, he hunted for a friendly tree and found a stout chestnut that suited his purpose.

Even here he might not be safe from the Germans. The jaegers' short, heavy rifles didn't have the range of a Pennsylvania long rifle but were nearly as accurate. Roland remembered too, the skill of the German artillerymen. His fingers traced the scar along his cheek. *On the whole,* thought Roland, *I'd prefer to fight the British.*

Roland searched for a target. From his position in the tree, he could see that the Germans were a little island, separate from the main British forces. If the Americans could cut them off altogether, it would be the end of this skirmish.

Roland found his target, a jaeger who was also scanning the field for a target. *How strange,* he thought, *he doesn't even know I'm here, but I am his Death, hidden, like quicksand or a teetering boulder.*

Roland saw the jaeger pause and bring up his rifle. This brought him out of his daydreaming. The German was aiming at one of Roland's countrymen, perhaps a friend, perhaps Colonel Morgan or Caleb. He had to be destroyed. Roland squeezed the trigger and saw the rifle leap out of the German's hands as the bullet slammed into his shoulder. At the same moment, shouts filled the air and the American infantry charged.

Cannon roared. Musketry crackled. Smoke and dust filled the air. In moments Roland's view was blocked. But he could hear the action. Learned's artillery had to let up so they wouldn't hit their own men. That meant the cannon fire still going was the Germans', no doubt blasting grapeshot into the charging infantry. Cringing with each blast, Roland could hear moans come from the battlefield as men were cut to pieces by flying death. He could hear shouting in German, maybe even coming from the Baron himself.

After several minutes, the noise faded. Roland realized the Americans must have fallen back. A few minutes more and the smoke lessened. Then, once again, he could look into the

German ranks. The men were nervous. They had learned that when the smoke cleared, the American riflemen went into action with their "Widow and Orphan-makers."

Roland checked for cannon aimed his way, but the artillery was being shifted around. The entire German position was in movement. Roland could see they had fallen back. Not much, and they were still in tight formation, but back. Once again, he scanned for a target. Then he saw the Baron.

Roland raised his rifle. But a movement at the edge of his vision made him flinch and stop. There, right in the midst of the battle walked a deer with two fawns. The fighting must have driven them from their hiding place. Now the panic-stricken doe was trying to lead her fawns to safety. They ran first at the Germans, then toward the American line. Then they retreated again and vanished into the woods below Roland's tree.

Roland again raised his rifle and brought the Baron into his sights. At the last second, he lowered it again. It was well known that the baron's wife and three children had accompanied him on this campaign. As Roland had been ready to fire, an image of them weeping over the Baron's dead body had come into his head. When Roland blinked it away the little German was giving orders to an artillery officer. Roland's rifle barrel shifted to the left.

"I'm sorry;" said Roland aloud," but I don't know who you are." Roland's rifle roared and the artilleryman fell over his cannon, dead.

Roland had been spotted. He could see men pointing in his direction and several jaegers scurried from their positions and aimed toward his tree. If he moved to reload, they would have a shot at him. If he kept still, he wouldn't be a target, but he'd be useless. He risked it and reloaded. Shots rang out and he could hear bullets hissing through the leaves of his tree. If he was lucky, he was outside the effective range of the German rifles. Also, he crouched still somewhat hidden by the leaves of the tree. The Germans, however, were standing in the open.

Roland leaned out to shoot. He aimed at the group of jaegers shooting at him. He fired. The powder flared, a flash in the pan. Rattled by his misfire, Roland bungled his reloading.

Again, shots rang out. Roland felt a burning sensation in his leg and realized he'd been shot. A mere graze, but a trickle of blood was staining his breeches above the knee. It was nothing to worry him and he continued to reload. But there was no chance to shoot. With a thunderous boom, American cannon fire fell upon the Germans, once again filling the air with smoke and dirt and bodies. Another infantry assault would soon follow.

The end of the artillery pummeling was followed by the infantry charge. Roland listened. Again, the Americans pulled back. As the smoke cleared, Roland could see that again, the Germans had withdrawn. The Americans had breached the German line and forced them back. The Germans had reformed and repulsed the American attack. But their ranks were dwindling.

Roland wasted no time. The Germans were falling out of range and if they moved before he got a shot off, he'd have to come down from his tree and advance before he could get in range again. A careless jaeger was his victim. Roland saw him go down but couldn't tell if it was a killing shot.

Before he could reload, Roland heard activity in the woods all around him. A mixture of riflemen and infantry had moved up. That could only mean Learned was preparing to press the issue and move up on the Germans again. Roland dropped from his tree and joined the others.

They moved along the German flank and Roland could see the retreating British come into view. They were still in a full retreat but organized. An officer on a horse galloped back and forth, shouting instructions. With a start, Roland realized that it was Gentleman Johnny himself.

Burgoyne was on his horse, trying to see through the smoke to plan his next move. The cannon fire and shouting made it difficult for him to give orders and he had to ride his horse back and forth to make himself noticed. Both wings of his attack had been beaten back by the rebels. It would now take all his command skills to make it back to the redoubt. American infantry pressed in again from both sides and Burgoyne's horse went down as a volley blasted the area. He rose, sullied but unharmed. His hat and coat were riddled with holes.

The Ghosts of Saratoga · 127

Still holding the line for the retreat, Baron vonRiedesel looked over the battleground. To his left and right, the British troops had collapsed and fallen back toward the redoubts. But he had received no orders to withdraw. More and more Americans moved into attack position with every passing minute.

von Riedesel shook his head. Snipers hidden in the trees picked off his men without ever showing themselves. Even their infantry moved in and out of the woods like wild animals. He'd never fought such enemies. It seemed as if they were a part of the land itself.

It was too late now to understand the American rebels. If the situation didn't change his men would soon be surrounded and slaughtered. He was planning a retreat path when something across the field caught his eye.

An American General on a tall horse had appeared on the field. At his approach, the American troops cheered and then pressed at the Germans harder than ever. Benedict Arnold had returned to the battlefield.

CHAPTER FIFTEEN - BATTLE OF BEMIS HEIGHTS PART 2

Arnold could stand it no longer. Gates had relieved him of his command, and he was an officer without troops. But he was still a born soldier. Muttering "No man can keep me in my tent today," he charged onto the field, ready to fight on his own if he needed to. Even in the chaos of the battle, he was an easy figure to recognize, and men moved to him, ready for his instructions.

Arnold's arrival spelled the end for the Germans. It took him moments to size up the situation. Without waiting for the artillery to move up, he hurled every available infantryman forward in a three-pronged assault on the Germans. Riedesel's men had fought with bravery, but the ferocity kindled in the American troops by Arnold's appearance was too much to resist. The Germans held bent and then cracked, retreating to the British center where Burgoyne was in command.

Arnold led the cheering infantry at the British. The Hessians didn't even have time to reorganize before the pursuing Americans were upon German and British alike.

Roland and Caleb were with Morgan when Arnold appeared. Morgan and Dearborn had flanked General Simon Fraser's troops and were pushing them back all the time. The riflemen worked the flanks, picking off officers or men at the edges of the formation. Meanwhile, Dearborn's infantry kept the retreating ranks occupied. With each backward movement by the British, the riflemen stretched their line, trying to cut off the retreat.

Things were hot around Roland. The American forces had moved close to the British ranks. They were well within English musket range. The air was full of lead. Roland preferred shooting from trees, but the action moved too fast. He had to stay on the ground to keep up. He and Caleb had moved along the British retreat and now they were more on the British side of the

The Ghosts of Saratoga · 129

skirmish line than the American.

Roland aimed and fired at an officer trying to organize his men into a disciplined withdrawal. His left arm was getting tired and the shot ran low. The officer fell to his knees, his leg shattered below the hip.

As Roland reloaded, the pursuit moved again and Colonel Morgan himself rushed by. A moment later Roland heard cheers as General Arnold charged by on his stallion. Roland hurried along behind them.

Ahead at a clearing the pursuit had slowed down. The riflemen were clustered in the trees along the edges while the infantry continued to press at the British retreat. Arnold was charging back and forth, shouting orders and sending charges. Roland was standing next to Colonel Morgan. Morgan paced glaring across the field at the British line. They had reformed and were now putting up stiff resistance. Roland could see a general on a gray horse riding up and down the British line at the same time as Arnold was riding along the American line. Moments later, Arnold rode up to Morgan, his face flushed and his sword out.

"Daniel!" shouted Arnold, "that man on the gray horse is a host in himself. He's the heart of the whole army and must be disposed of."

Morgan nodded and Arnold rode off, shouting orders. Morgan noticed Roland standing next to him.

"McCaffrey, find Tim Murphy and tell him to come here with all haste." Roland ran off.

Across the field, General Simon Fraser tried to rally his troops. He knew there was no way to win the day, but his men had the responsibility to provide a defense for General Burgoyne's retreat. The Americans were in hot pursuit. If his men couldn't slow them down, Burgoyne himself would be surrounded. The battle, and maybe even the war, would be lost. He spurred his horse along the line, encouraging his men.

Fraser's aide, seeing bullets fill the air, pleaded with him to dismount, but Fraser knew the men needed to see their commander. They gained courage from his example. He refused to come down from the horse.

The man was brave, Roland could see that. Whenever the ranks faltered, Fraser would ride to the spot. Seeing him seemed to give the men extra energy. It seemed to Roland he could see them standing taller at his approach. Fraser shouted encouragement, moved men to fill gaps, and coordinated their movements. Glancing up his own line, Roland saw Arnold doing all the same things, pausing only to glare across the field at Fraser.

It didn't take Roland long to find Tim Murphy, the best shot of all Morgan's men. He was the winner of the shooting contest. That seemed like a lifetime ago. They raced back to Morgan.

"Tim!" Morgan's voice roared even over the sounds of battle. He pointed over at Fraser on his gray horse. "That man is General Fraser. He is a gallant officer and I admire him, but he must be disposed of. Do your duty."

Murphy squinted through the haze of gun smoke at the man on the gray horse. Then he nodded.

"I need a good tree," Murphy said to Roland.

"I know the perfect place." replied Roland.

They both turned to Morgan.

"Well, for God's sake get going then! It's General Arnold's direct order!"

Roland stood fascinated. He couldn't decide whether to watch Murphy or Fraser. He twisted his head back and forth, his heart racing. Beside them, the battle was getting more intense as the British lines pulled together. Between the blasting of cannon, the crackle of muskets and the shouting of men, the roar of battle was deafening. Heavy smoke lay over the area. It was poor conditions for accurate shooting, yet Murphy seemed calm.

His first shot ripped off target, tearing through the reins of Fraser's horse. The General flinched, the horse reared, but Fraser stayed in the saddle. Murphy's second shot passed through the horse's mane. An aide reached up and grabbed at the horse's reins. The man shouted at Fraser, who shook his head. Murphy's third shot found its mark, tearing into the brave general's body below his stomach. He slumped, teetered and fell to the ground.

The effect on the British troops was immediate. Roland could see Fraser's fierce fighting men looking for direction. But there was no one who could take his place. The ranks, coordinated and confident seconds ago, now showed gaps and indecision. Arnold too saw the result of Murphy's shot. Waving his sword as musket balls zoomed by, he ordered another charge.

This time there was no stopping the American surge. The British line, better trained in the tactics of a bayonet charge, tried to hold, but the sheer numbers and determination of the Americans was too much for them. The resistance turned into a rout. Even in retreat, the disciplined troops refused to panic. They remained in ranks as they backed toward the Balcarres Redoubt.

Roland raced along with the American advance. The center of the battlefield was no place for a young rifleman. He moved along the wooded areas trying to get into position to fire on the retreating British flank. The battle slowed down as the British held their ground again. Roland used the pause and climbed into a friendly tree.

The view from the tree stopped any thoughts of shooting. He stared in horror at the violence below. Rows of men hacked at each other with bayonets. Muskets were fired at point blank range. Tomahawks, knives and bare hands were all used as Americans, British and Germans grappled in the smoky autumn afternoon. The dead and wounded were trampled underneath as the living took their place in line.

In the distance, he could see the massive earth wall of the Balcarres Redoubt. To the west were the log walls of the Breymann Redoubt. In between the redoubts were the cabins manned by Canadians. Roland had scouted these sites several times over the last three weeks but hadn't seen it all laid out from above before.

The battleground itself was obscured by the smoke. Through the clear spots, Roland could make out what was happening. The British were in full retreat. They were falling back to the Balcarres Redoubt, pressed by large numbers of American infantry. The Breymann Redoubt also fell under assault by the rebel army. Some cannon had been moved to the high ground above it and were blasting at the log walls.

The cannon firing ceased for a few minutes, *they're all overheated,* thought Roland. The break allowed the smoke to clear. That was always the signal for American riflemen to go into action. As soon as it was clear enough to sight a target, they began their attack. Roland continued to stare at the action. He knew he should load and fire but pulled out his spyglass to look over the British lines.

He could see several officers. By now he could recognize many of them. The German, vonRiedesel, was there in the thick of the action with his disciplined German troops. Even under retreat, they were in perfect order, moving as if they had one mind. As a man fell, another moved into his place. They were retreating, true, but still they moved ranks up to fire volleys. The British General Phillips was also there. Roland didn't like that. Phillips commanded the artillery and every time Roland saw him on the battlefield, the air was soon full of grapeshot. Even as he watched, Roland could see Phillips signaling artillerymen up to help cover the retreat.

A third officer was there in the thick of it, too. Gentleman Johnny himself. Roland thought of General Gates, sitting in the safety of Fort Neilson. Gates had managed the strategy well, but the man had never seen a moment of the battles in person. He sat receiving reports and studying maps and sending out orders. Roland had to admire Burgoyne, here in the danger zone, letting his men see his courage. *Still,* thought Roland, *he is the enemy, THE Enemy.* He put away his spyglass and pulled out his powder pouch.

It was a long shot, at the limit of Roland's range. And the man was on his horse, a moving target. Roland thought of Tim Murphy's amazing shot. If he could do the same, it might end the battle here and now. Roland raised his rifle. His chance came when Burgoyne stopped to shout orders to one of his officers. Roland fired.

Burgoyne jerked back as his horse reared, and they both went over on the ground. Roland held his breath and tried to see what was going on, as men were scurrying all over the place.

The Ghosts of Saratoga · 133

Then he saw Burgoyne stand, brushing dirt from his soiled uniform and turning around as if to glare at whoever had the daring to shoot at him. Roland reloaded. But before he could finish two aides grabbed at the general and rushed him back into the ranks.

Roland had forgotten about Phillips and vonRiedesel while he had been concentrating on Burgoyne. The roar of cannon brought them back to mind. Once again, Roland was clinging to a tree as grapeshot peppered the battlefield. A few strays came his way this time, but the barrage targeted the infantry. Then, to his amazement, the Germans and British made a countercharge at the Americans.

It was well organized. The pursuing Americans had fallen out of formation in their excitement. The charge was well across the field before the officers could even find their platoons. Surprised, the American force, though much greater in number, gave ground as it tried to reorganize.

The charge brought the British and German infantry into range of the riflemen, but the wily Phillips and the German Pausch had turned the guns into the trees. Grape thrashed around Roland in a murderous rain. Jaeger riflemen were also pouring their fire into the trees.

Roland peeked out after a cannon burst to see what was going on. As he did a German rifle shot struck his gun and it clattered to the ground. Roland stared down at it. The battle had moved near his tree, but he was useless without a weapon. He climbed down to retrieve it.

As he picked up his rifle, Roland heard a harsh breath and turned to see a German soldier bearing down on him with a bayonet. The German thrust, but Roland blocked it with his rifle. The German made another move and Roland saw his rifle yanked out of his hands, hooked by the German's blade. He reached behind for his pistol, hoping he had remembered to load it. But the German was quick. He made another thrust at Roland, the blade grazing his shoulder. Before Roland could react, the German snapped his musket back the other way, the barrel whacking Roland in the forehead and knocking him to the ground. The blow had stunned him but he kept his senses and rolled as he hit. The bayonet thumped into the ground next him.

Roland rolled again, bumped against a tree trunk and raised up on one arm. To his surprise, the German was no longer after him. Instead, the bayonet pointed at a large man armed with a tomahawk. It was Caleb.

The two men circled each other in a death dance. The German feinted and Caleb took a swipe at him with the tomahawk and missed. They circled again. The German lunged. Caleb caught the edge of the bayonet with his tomahawk. But the tomahawk wasn't Caleb's most dangerous weapon. The German realized this too late as the Irishman's fist struck his jaw.

Caleb landed a terrible blow. Roland could hear the crack as if it were a rifle shot. The German flew backward as if he had been hit with a cannonball. He crashed against a tree and bounced off. He turned, took a step and fell face down and motionless. Caleb helped Roland to his feet.

"A close one, child." said Caleb.

"Too close, I'm still shaking," replied Roland.

"Are you bad hurt?" asked Caleb

Roland brushed at his shoulder. "A scratch, but my head's throbbing like the devil."

Caleb spoke but his words were drowned out by deafening shouts as the Albany County militia poured through the woods. They were followed by more brigades. The Americans had reformed under Arnold. Now they turned on the British with their fiercest attack yet. Caleb and Roland watched as the force charged by.

"So many," said Roland.

"Aye, this might be it lad, the final charge. I'd sure hate to miss it."

"As would I."

"Then let's get our guns and join them."

"I'm afraid my rifle's damaged," said Roland.

Caleb rubbed his chin. "Ah, I lost mine a ways back. Here," He walked over and picked up the German's musket. "A butcher's weapon, to be sure, but better than bare hands. Can you use one?" He handed it to Roland.

"I can shoot one, sure. But I've never used a bayonet."

The Ghosts of Saratoga

"Let's hope it don't come to that. Be off, I'm sure there'll be a spare musket for me along the way."

He was right. There were dead soldiers, British and German, American too, all over the place. Caleb and Roland chased the British force to the Balcarres Redoubt. The American forces had pursued and were attacking the redoubt itself.

The Balcarres Redoubt was made of thick earthen walls, built the right height to hide behind and shoot over. Cannon had been put into position to defend the redoubt against an infantry charge. The ground had been cleared for a distance from the walls. Any attack had to come over an unprotected killing field.

Orders or no orders, it was General Benedict Arnold who now held command of the American troops on the battlefield. Gates could take away his official status, but in the heat of battle, no other man could pull this army together. Continental soldiers and militiaman alike responded to him. The battle frenzy held him now.

Arnold knew better than any man how difficult it would be to take the Balcarres Redoubt. But he also knew it was the only thing blocking their path to the Great Redoubt and the last British refuge. If Balcarres could be taken, the day would be won, and the British invasion force crushed. The bitter taste of the defeats at Quebec and Valcour was still in Arnold's mouth and he was ready to sweeten it with victory.

The riflemen split and spread to the edges of the woods. When the British had cleared the forest to create an open fighting ground, they had underestimated the range of the Americans' rifles. Morgan's men continued to pick off any man who showed himself above the redoubt embankment.

Infantrymen now, Roland and Caleb joined up with some men they recognized and fell into rank. The order was given and with a cheer, the infantry charged.

This gave a view of the battle Roland had not experienced before. They pounded across the open ground, stopping only to reload. There was no time to aim and with the dubious accuracy of the musket, no point. Musket balls were whizzing by as he charged the redoubt. The roar of cannon shook the ground and grapeshot once again filled the field. This time there was no tree to hide behind. A piece of the shot skimmed Roland's head, taking off his hat and grazing his scalp. Ahead of him, a soldier took a full load of grapeshot. It lifted him off his feet and threw him back toward Roland, his ruined body lifeless by the time it hit the ground.

More English guns battered the charging patriot force. At last, it became folly to continue. A retreat was called. The tired infantry dropped to the ground out of artillery range.

"That was horrible!" gasped Roland.

Caleb nodded. "Aye, lad, that it was. I don't know if we can take that dirt fortress without more men."

They had not yet caught their breath when they again heard the roar of cannon, this time American. Arnold had somehow moved several heavy guns to the front. The men stood to watch.

A cannonball plowed into the side of the redoubt. Dirt flew into the air and the Americans cheered. An officer rushed through the ranks.

"Form up, boys! We'll soften 'em up with the guns and hit 'em again!"

Caleb looked at Roland, his face tight and dirty. Then he broke into a grin.

"You are a sight, child!" he laughed. "I don't know which is more tattered, your clothes or your body. At least you had the sense to have that hat shot off."

Roland had to laugh at himself. It was true, he was a mess. Head, shoulder, leg, and God only knew what bruises would show up tomorrow if lived to see them.

The charge sounded and the infantry once again hit the open. Once, twice, three times Arnold hurled the American forces at the Balcarres. Each time the brave Americans responded. But each time the British troops hung tough. The advantage of their walls and artillery outweighed the numerical advantage of the Americans. Arnold called off the attack.

Dead tired, and bloodied, Roland and Caleb trudged along behind Arnold's horse with the other infantrymen. Roland had stopped being able to think after that first charge. He moved where the other men moved, charged when they charged and prayed he would survive.

Following Arnold's orders, they found themselves again reunited with Morgan and Dearborn's men. Arnold was talking with Morgan when he rose higher on his horse and looked off to the east. There was Learned's brigade, marching up, tired but game. Arnold rode off toward them, and, as he approached a wild cheer went up from the men. A few minutes later, Arnold came galloping back and talked with Morgan and Dearborn, who shouted orders.

Morgan's men, including Roland and Caleb, went with Learned's brigade, now commanded by Arnold. Dearborn's men moved off to the west.

It didn't take Roland long to identify Arnold's new target. It was the Breymann Redoubt. Morgan sent them out in a flanking position along the eastern edge of the redoubt. Dearborn moved his infantry into position to attack the main front of the log wall, sweeping down from the heights and across the open. Learned's men would drive straight through the Canadian cabins and onto the Germans unprotected flank. Dearborn's men began the attack. They had already made several assaults on the Breymann redoubt and Dearborn was reluctant to try again. But with Arnold commanding, he would give it another try. His tired men charged once more.

Learned's orders were to wait until the cabins had been cleared. Then, with Morgan's men attacking on one flank and Learned's on the other, the redoubt would fall. So, for now, Roland had to watch and wait.

With Learned's infantry leading the charge, Arnold crashed into the cabins like a thunderstorm. The Canadians were caught by surprise. They fired one volley and ran. With the cabins taken, the flank was open. The Americans regrouped, and Arnold led the assault on the redoubt. At that moment, Morgan gave the order and Roland charged with the other men.

Roland could see the Breymann redoubt was finished. Attacked on three sides, the Germans were caught in a crossfire. Still, they put up the stiff resistance Roland had seen again and again from them. The end came when Arnold charged into the redoubt itself on his horse. With that, the Americans poured in like water. Morgan's men encountered little resistance. Arnold was creating absolute chaos in the redoubt by the time Roland arrived. He was swinging his sword and shouting. The crazed horse was trampling Germans under its hooves.

There was loud shouting in German at the opposite end of the redoubt. Soldiers were rushing to escape. But vonBreymann himself was blocking their path. He was shouting in anger at his fleeing men. As one tried to slip past him, vonBreymann struck him down with his heavy sword.

The other Germans backed away from their commander. One of them turned back into the redoubt. He cast a glance at the American infantry pouring in and the wild officer charging on his berserk stallion. Then he turned back to vonBreymann, leveled his musket and shot him down. The Germans bolted from the redoubt.

Roland got careless watching vonBreymann and found himself in the path of a retreating German. He slashed at Roland with his bayonet. Roland dodged and thrust in retaliation with all his might. The blade hit the German solid between the ribs. The man spun around, and the musket twisted from Roland's hands. Now he was in the middle of hand to hand combat without a weapon. Remembering his pistol, he pulled it out. At this range, it would be effective.

The stamping of horse's hooves nearby made Roland turn. Arnold was still storming about the redoubt. The Germans were in absolute panic. Many of them now realized who was leading this attack. Arnold's horse knocked a German to the ground. The horse reared up and the terrified man fired his musket. The horse screamed, crashed to the ground and rolled. Roland could hear Arnold cry out.

The horse, still thrashing, was pulled off. Arnold, in obvious agony, was carried out the way. A Massachusetts soldier aimed his gun at the German.

"No! Don't hurt him!" shouted Arnold. "He is a fine fellow! He was only doing his duty."

Roland looked at the state of things in the redoubt. It was full of Americans, as the Germans were in full retreat to the Great

Redoubt. He saw Caleb with a group of infantrymen, racing out of the redoubt in pursuit. Roland followed, pistol in hand.

Ahead Caleb was gaining on a German soldier. The man stopped and whirled around. He thrust at Caleb with his bayonet. Caleb crumpled and fell to the ground. At this, the German threw his musket aside and raised his hands in surrender. Roland and several American soldiers rushed up.

Roland saw Caleb lying bloody on the ground and knew he was dead. He raised his pistol and walked to the German. He pressed the barrel against the German's forehead. The man pleaded in his native tongue.

"You Hessian bastard!" he shouted. The man closed his eyes. Roland curled his finger around the trigger when a hand touched his shoulder.

"You're a soldier, McCaffrey, not an executioner. Don't do it."

For a moment he held his grip on the pistol. Then he closed his eyes and let his arm fall. He turned to Daniel Morgan.

"He killed him, Colonel, he killed Caleb!"

"Nonsense boy," said Morgan. "It takes more than a mercenary's bayonet to kill an Irishman. You should know that by now."

Roland leaned past Morgan as two men helped Caleb to his feet. Roland ran over to him, not caring about the tears streaking his filthy face.

"It's a nasty cut, Rollie boy, but I'll be all right," chucked Caleb. "The blade bounced off when it hit this." He pulled out his whiskey flask and took a sip. It was leaking where the edge of the bayonet had struck. "How's the General? I heard he went down."

Roland wiped the tears off his face. His hands were shaking with emotion.

"His horse rolled on him. I think his leg is broke. Broke bad."

Despite his best efforts to control himself, Roland put his arms around the big Irishman, his head resting on the massive chest.

"Caleb...Sergeant...I... I thought...thank God you're alive!"

"And you, child?" asked Caleb, patting Roland's head.

Roland smiled. "I'm well, Sergeant, I'm well."

From the Balcarres Redoubt, Burgoyne had seen the fall of the Breymann Redoubt. The battle was over, the invasion was over, and with it, his career. With the Breymann overrun, the Americans had a clear path to flank both Balcarres and the Great Redoubt. They had overwhelming numbers and the flush courage of victory. The day was lost. If he didn't act now his army would also be lost, surrounded and forced to its knees, defeated by this ragtag mob of bumpkins.

Word had not reached him yet of Arnold's fall. His last reports said that Arnold was in effective command of the American forces. The fiery American was not a man who would settle for taking the field and holding it. He would regroup and come at Balcarres from every direction. Even fortified, no redoubt could withstand that kind of assault. Already he could see Breymann's cannons being turned his way.

Burgoyne gave the only order he could, a full withdrawal from Balcarres to the Great Redoubt, his last stronghold. Perhaps he could yet save the remains of his invasion force. The way back to Ticonderoga might still be open. All thoughts of Albany were tossed aside.

As darkness fell, the American forces moved in to occupy the Breymann Redoubt. A few groups of skirmishers harassed the British as they pulled back across the ravine to the Great Redoubt. General Arnold was carried back to the hospital. General Fraser was carried to a nearby house. Baroness vonRiedesel would tend to him until he died a few hours later.

Gates sat savoring his victory. He had stopped the British invasion from Canada and handed the British their most serious defeat in the war so far. As in the last battle, British losses on the day totaled over 600. His were nearer to 100. Not only did he hold the field, but he had driven the foe back. He would let his usual caution be his guide, but Gates realized he might do more than win this battle; he might capture Burgoyne and his army. A complete surrender. What a victory that would be! Such a victory could not be ignored by the Continental Congress. Perhaps he would be promoted to co-commander alongside Washington. And why not? What had that amateur done to compare with this victory?

Roland went out that night with a group of men searching for American wounded. They also checked the bodies of the dead for letters or diaries to send to their families. Roland could see the British losses had been considerable. In spots their dead lay in piles.

As the moon rose, the sound of bagpipes came rolling over the battleground. They were playing the "Mist Covered Mountains." Roland's party stopped and listened till the tune was done.

"Must be some of Fraser's men." said the man next to Roland.

"He was a brave man," said Roland, "I saw him fall."

"They say it was Tim Murphy took him down. Is that true?"

" Tis," said Roland," and such a shot as I've never seen."

"A strange fate it is that watches over the likes of us and drops a man like that, eh?" said the soldier.

"It is, yet in the end, he was only a man, same's you and me. Wealth, fame and a fancy uniform won't stop a bullet any more than this buckskin."

The man tilted his head at Roland as if he were trying to figure out who he was. Then he gazed off toward the sound of bagpipes starting up again. He smiled and nodded.

"I reckon you're right at that."

Roland stopped by the hospital to see how Caleb fared. He was already bandaged and under Bridget's care. She leaped to her feet when she saw Roland. His musket fell to the ground as she jumped into his arms.

"Da told me you were all right, but I thought to never see you again. What a beating you give them today Roland. My Roland."

Roland closed his eyes and let his head rest against hers as he held her tight. Later, after she had patched up his wounds, they strolled together under the moonlight. She was uncharacteristically quiet. Shy, he hesitated and then grasped her hand.

She did not pull it away.

"I think something important happened here today, Bridget. Something the rest of the world, not England, will stand up and take notice of. We licked 'em, licked 'em good. They weren't lackeys, either. They were top troops, Grenadiers, Hessians, you know. And look at all the folks that pulled together to make it happen. Nobody worried today about who was from New York and who was from New England. It was Americans, fighting for America."

He lifted his arms toward the stars peeking through the clouds.

"Do you have any idea Bridget, how many men I've killed here?" said Roland, lowering his outstretched arms. Bridget shook her head but remained silent. Roland tore his gaze from the sky.

"Nor do I. Can you believe that? Human beings with families, dreams, hopes for the future. But no more because of me."

"Rollie, I... I don't know what to say. You've fought for your country. You've done the dirty work for the rest of us. Yes, they're dead but..."

"They haunt me, Bridget. Every night they come. And it seems like every day I add to their number. I'm afraid to go to sleep tonight, afraid of what I'll dream."

Bridget looked up at him and smiled.

"Why don't you dream about me?"

Roland laid awake a long time before sleep came to him. He was exhausted and sore, but his mind wouldn't slow down. The day's events kept racing through; Caleb, Bridget, Arnold, Fraser, vonBreymann, Tim Murphy, the men he'd killed. His thoughts turned to the German commander, von Riedesel.

Why didn't I kill him? thought Roland. *He's an enemy, the leader of the Hessian mercenaries. I had him in my sights. It was an easy shot. Now, he's still alive. He could kill me tomorrow. Or Caleb. He might order an artillery attack that could kill Bridget! Why didn't I kill him? Wallace Travers wouldn't have hesitated.*

The memory of Travers returning from the Hessian camp

covered in blood came into his mind. Roland's heart stopped and his eyes grew wide.

Is that what I'm becoming? A pure killer? An Angel of Death?

Roland could keep his eyes open no longer. As he slept, the ghosts came. But this time they took him to the enemy camp, to the tent of Baron von Riedesel. There stood the stocky Hessian general. His arms were wrapped around his wife. Their three tiny daughters hugged his knees.

CHAPTER SIXTEEN - SURRENDER

On October 8th, the American forces moved up to the Great Ravine. Both day and night, snipers kept up a continuous harassment of the British camp. Gates moved his artillery into place to pound the Great Redoubt. On the 9th, Burgoyne pulled his army out in the pouring rain, taking advantage of the weather to avoid another battle. As they moved north, he camped his force at General Schuyler's summer mansion. Meanwhile, the Americans crossed the Hudson to occupy the highlands of the eastern bank.

Burgoyne paused in his retreat to consider his strategy. Gates declined to engage in another infantry battle. Instead, he poured artillery fire on the British position. He had captured much of their ammunition and many of their cannon, and he was putting it all to good use. His forces had cut the British off from both supplies and escape. Trapped in a circle of artillery, Burgoyne's once proud army was pounded day and night.

Finding his army of 3,500 surrounded by an American force now numbering over 15,000, even Burgoyne could take no more. On the morning of October 14, 1777, he sent word to Gates that he would surrender on the 16th.

On the day of the surrender, Roland was with a group of American soldiers under Major James Wilkinson, Gates's aide. Several scouts had been sent along with Wilkinson's party to keep an eye out for any British treachery. It was this party's task to go to the British camp and escort General Burgoyne to General Gates for the formal surrender.

When they arrived at the British camp, Burgoyne and his officers came out from Burgoyne's tent in their best uniforms, brushed and polished. In contrast, Wilkinson and his group

The Ghosts of Saratoga · 145

were still in their battle dress, the rigors of the last month showed in the wear and tear of their clothing.

Roland maneuvered himself into position on the return trip where he could listen to Burgoyne and Wilkinson as they talked. They exchanged pleasantries regarding the weather and the beauty of the countryside and the river. At one point, Burgoyne slowed and pointed over the river.

"Is it possible to ford at this spot?" he asked Wilkinson.

Wilkinson narrowed his eyes at the British general. Roland glanced back and forth between the two men. *Is he still thinking of trying to escape us?* he wondered. *Would he really try to cross the Hudson with his starving, shattered army?*

"Certainly sir," replied Wilkinson," but do you observe the people on the opposite shore?" He pointed to the American encampment on the eastern bank.

"Yes," sighed Burgoyne, "I have seen them for too long."

At the American camp, General Gates was there to meet them. Wilkinson made the formal introductions. Burgoyne raised his hat and made a slight bow.

"The fortunes of war, General Gates, have made me your prisoner.

The Battle of Saratoga was over.

On the morning of October 20, 1777, Roland went to see Caleb and Bridget. He was under full pack.

"So, child, are you off with Colonel Morgan then?" asked Caleb. He knew that Morgan had asked Roland to sign on as a permanent scout with the riflemen.

"No Sergeant, I've seen enough death for a while. I'm headed home first. I'm to meet up with Colonel Morgan next month at a place in Pennsylvania called Valley Forge"

"Och, I'm glad to hear it, lad. I wish you well." He reached out, and Roland disappeared in the embrace of his massive arms.

"I'll miss you, Caleb. Thanks for saving my life. All the times." A tear trickled from Roland's eye and he brushed it away like it was a stinging insect.

"I'm sorry. I feel like a baby. All the death I've seen and the men I've killed, and I still bawl like a little girl."

"Don't apologize child. It's a rare man who can do what you've done and still have feelings at all, let alone tears."

Roland smiled and nodded.

"Be well, Sergeant. I hope we'll meet again."

"I have a feeling we will, Rollie." He smiled up into the sky. "I think it's written up there."

Roland turned to Bridget.

"And where are you bound, then lass?"

She smiled. "I'm headed back to Albany. And I expect you to visit before you head off to Pennsylvania."

Bridget kissed her father and walked with Roland down to the boats, where she would board, and head down the Hudson. As she stepped to the dock, they stared uncertainly at each other for a moment and then kissed. Bridget straightened herself, blushing.

"Take care of yourself, Roland McCaffrey."

"And you, Miss O'Connor. 'Til the day."

Her eyes sparkled for a moment and then she was gone. Roland stood and watched the flotilla depart, remembering another flotilla arriving not that long ago. Crown Point seemed another life and another planet.

Roland turned and headed for home, carrying his new rifle, a gift from Colonel Morgan. At the edge of the encampment, he turned around. He paused and spoke to his new traveling companions.

"Let's go, boys, time to head for home," he said to his ghosts, the ghosts of Saratoga.

Caleb watched until Roland disappeared into the woods. He turned around, staring into the dead eyes of the men he had killed. He raised his whiskey flask and nodded to them. With a gulp, he drained the flask. He tossed it away and scowled at his ghosts.

"Come on mates, we'd best be off."

The Ghosts of Saratoga · 147

Slowly, silently, they formed into ranks and followed him across the camp.

ABOUT THE AUTHORS

DAVID DAMPF has been a middle school social studies teacher for the past 28 years. He has a bachelor's degree from SUNY Potsdam with a major in history and secondary education and a master's degree in reading from SUNY Cortland. Since he believes that understanding history is essential to being an educated, thoughtful adult; he has spent his life telling stories that make history come alive. He lives in Oneida, New York, with his family.

DAVID R. OSSONT has worked as a musician, a Fish and Wildlife Technician and for nearly three decades taught science to seventh and eighth graders. He received his college education from several colleges of the State University of New York. He has two children, Kyle and Hayley and lives with his wife Pam in upstate New York, not far from where the events of Ghosts of Saratoga take place.

ACKNOWLEDGEMENTS

We'd like to thank all the folks at Sunbury in general, and Chris Fenwick in particular. Your support and belief in our words brought our "Hey gang, let's put on a show!" type idea to fruition.

www.ingramcontent.com/pod-product-compliance
Lightning Source LLC
Chambersburg PA
CBHW051344040426
42453CB00007B/396